Beyond Death

BEYOND DEATH

THE GNOSTIC BOOK OF THE DEAD

Samael Aun Weor

GLORIAN
2010

Beyond Death
A Glorian Book / 2010

Originally published in Spanish as:
1. Beyond Death: Originally published in Spanish as "Más Allá de
La Muerte" (1970).
2. The Mysteries of Life and Death: Originally published in
Spanish as "Los Misterios de La Vida y de La Muerte" (1962).
3. The Book of the Dead: Originally published in Spanish as "El
Libro de Los Muertos" (1966).
4. A Talk on the Mysteries of Life and Death: from a lecture.

ISBN-13: 978-1-934206-33-1

Glorian Publishing is a non-profit organization. All proceeds go
to further the distribution of these books. For more information,
visit our websites.

glorian.info
gnosticbooks.org
gnosticradio.org
gnosticteachings.org

Contents

A Talk on the Mysteries of Life and Death

Editor's Introduction

Although most of us prefer to avoid the topic of death, it is a simple fact that we must come to terms with, especially if we are serious about our spiritual development. For the serious aspirant to the Light, death ceases to be a source of fear or uncertainty. Instead, death is revealed to be what it truly is: a door, an integral part of existence, and even a method for acheiving greater degrees of development.

This book collects together several small books by Samael Aun Weor that were originally published in Spanish. We have organized them more or less according to their depth and complexity, beginning with the most accessible and ending with the most sophisticated. The reader will discover here that there is more to death than the end of life, and, we hope, that the reader will deepen their own sense of life, and strive to live it better.

In his teachings, Samael Aun Weor emphasized death as one of the key factors of the path. Death, birth, and sacrifice are the three factors that reside at the heart of every true reflection of the method to awaken the consciousness, whether we all that method a religion or not, for every true path to the Light comes from that same source and carries within it the same essential knowledge, even if the names and faces appear different. Samael Aun Weor called this root knowledge or religion "Gnosis," from a Greek word that means "knowledge." He clarified what has always been taught in the core or heart of every religion: the path to the Light is exact, and only what is pure can ascend there; everything else must die. Thus, by making ourselves pure and "one with the Light" we naturally rise to the heights of existence. The means to acheive this is found in the death of all that is impure within us, the birth of that which is pure and light, and finally, ultimately, by sacrificing to help others do the same.

Through the death of impurity, purity is freed and can rise. Through acts of sacrifice and love, the ascension of purity is accelerated and intensified. This is the heart message of every religion, and the choice is ours to make: to remain trapped in impurity and ignorance, or to free ourselves from the cage of suffering, pain, and death, and thereby acheive the ultimate purpose of existence. By preparing now for our unavoidable death, rather than that transition being a cause for fear, pain, and uncertainty, we can make of something wondrous, divine, and important. For the Gnostic, death is the crown of life, and the entryway into something new.

Beyond Death

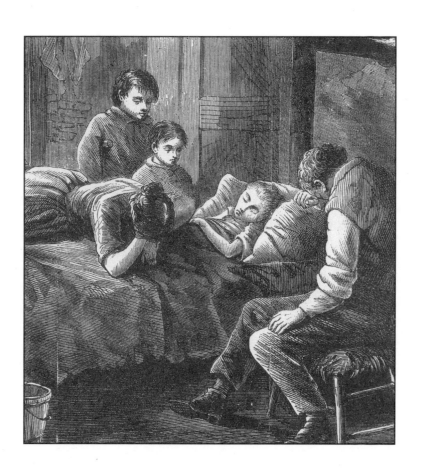

Chapter One
Physical Death

1. What is physical death?

Samael Aun Weor: The cessation of all organic functions, to decease.

2. What is beyond death?

Samael Aun Weor: Death is something profoundly significant. By discovering what death is in itself, we will know the secret of life. That which continues beyond the sepulcher can be only known by people who have awakened their consciousness. Your consciousness is asleep, and therefore you cannot know what is beyond death. Theories are as many as the sands of the sea, thus each one has his own opinion, but what is important is to experience in a direct manner that which belongs to the mysteries beyond the grave. I can assure you that the souls of the deceased live within the beyond of this great nature.

3. Why does fear towards death exist?

Samael Aun Weor: Fear towards death exists because of ignorance; we always fear what we do not know. Yet, when the consciousness awakens, ignorance disappears; then, fear towards the unknown ceases to exist.

4. We know that after death the physical body disintegrates in the grave, but what happens or where does the soul go?

Samael Aun Weor: The soul of the deceased continues to live within the superior dimensions of nature. This means in fact that the disembodied souls can see the sun, the moon, the stars, the rivers, the valleys, the mountains, just like we, but in a more splendid manner.

5. Is it true that after living a wicked and libertine type of life, if we repent at the moment of death, then our soul can be saved?

Samael Aun Weor: All the doors are closed for the unworthy, except one: the door of repentance. It is clear that if we repent, even if it is at the last moment, then we can be assisted in order to amend our errors.

6. Why do some come like ghosts to this world after physically passing away?

   Samael Aun Weor: It is good to know that parallel universes exist within this planet—regions of the fourth dimension and beyond—where the deceased live; such apparently invisible worlds intermingle with ours without confusion.

7. Where does the soul of a human being who takes his own life go?

   Samael Aun Weor: Those who commit suicide suffer a great deal after their death, and live here and now yet in the region of dead, and after a certain period of time they return into a new maternal womb and appear again in this valley of tears. Then, when their new body arrives again at the age in which they committed suicide in the past, they die again, but against their will, perhaps at a moment in which they are more captivated by life.

8. Is the spirit the same as the soul?

   Samael Aun Weor: The Spirit *Is* and the Soul is attained. They are therefore different.

9. Do animals and plants have soul?

   Samael Aun Weor: Yes, they do. The souls of plants are known in all universal legends with the names of fairies, etc. The souls of animals are innocent creatures. Let us be aware that if we take the last letter, the "L", from the word animal we then have the word "anima" (soul).

10. Does a superior judgment exist after death, and if it does, who executes it?

    Samael Aun Weor: After death, we review the life that we just finished; we relive it in a retrospective manner, by means of the intelligence and the heart. After such a retrospection has concluded, we then must appear before the Courts of God. The Angels of the Law are called amongst the Eastern people the Lords of Karma; they judge us according to our deeds. The outcome of such a judgment could be that we may return again into a new womb in order to appear again immediately in this physical world, or we may enter into a kind of vacation within the worlds of the light and happiness, or finally—regrettably—we could be obligated to enter into the interior of the Earth, within its infradimensions, with all of its pains and displeasures.

11. When a baby dies at the moment of his birth, where does his soul go?

Samael Aun Weor: It is written that the souls of babies enter into Limbo, the region of dead; thereafter they leave Limbo in order to enter into a new womb and thus to reappear again in this world.

12. What is the cause for a baby to die at the moment of his birth?

Samael Aun Weor: It is because of the law of destiny: the parents needed to suffer such a hard lesson, since in their former lives they were cruel to their children, thus through this suffering they improve, they learn about love.

13. Are the funeral masses that are performed after people's death an aid to the soul?

Samael Aun Weor: Any ritual is an aid to the souls of the deceased; it is clear that the prayers from the sorrowful ones give consolation to the souls of the deceased.

Chapter Two

Beyond the Tomb

1. Why is it that at the moment of death some cry, others sing, and others smile?

Samael Aun Weor: The answer to this question is divided in three parts:

FIRST: It is written that one is born crying and dies crying.

SECOND: There are cases in which the agonizing one sings when remembering happy moments of the past.

THIRD: Some smile (although this is not very common), possibly remembering likeable scenes of their existence.

2. Who commands the soul to leave the body so that it can be buried?

Samael Aun Weor: An Angel of Death arrives at the bed of the dying one at the moment in which he exhales his last breath; there are legions of Angels of Death. So, any of these funeral Angels cuts the silver cord or thread of life that connects the soul to the physical body. The dying ones usually see such Angels adopting a spectral appearance. The scythe with which these deities are represented is certainly real—such an instrument of work serves exactly so that such deities can cut the thread of existence.

3. What do the souls of the deceased eat and how do they pay for what they consume?

Samael Aun Weor: Here in Mexico we celebrate The Day of the Dead on November first and second of every year. On such a day people visit the pantheon, place lit candles at the tombs, and place on plates, pots, glasses, etc., the foods and drinks that pleased the deceased ones when they were alive. It is customary for many of those people to later eat the meals left at the tombs; however, whoever has some psychic sensitivity can verify that such food lacks the "vital principle." The simple people think—and they are right about it—that their dear, deceased ones feed

themselves with those meals. Indeed, there is no doubt
that the deceased ones eat—not the physical part of that
food, but, we would say, the ethereal part of such a food;
such a subtle aspect is unknown to physical sight, but per-
ceivable to clairvoyance. So, let us not forget that ethereal
food exists within any physical food, and that this is easily
assimilable for the deceased ones.

The deceased ones can also visit a restaurant in the physical world; they salute those who are physically alive, whose
subconsciousness will answer such a salutation. Thus,
the deceased ones request food, and it is obvious that the
internal ego of the owner of the restaurant will unconsciously bring to the table mental forms of plates and
foods similar to the ones that are physically consumed
in his restaurant; thus the deceased ones—seated in the
dining area—will eat of those "subtle meals" made with
essence of the mental world, they will pay with "mental
currency," and thereafter they will leave the restaurant.
In such conditions it is obvious that the deceased ones
continue thinking that they are physically alive. This can
be demonstrated by any person who has developed clairvoyance and other faculties of the soul.

4. Where do the deceased ones live?

Samael Aun Weor: For the first few days, the deceased ones live
in the house where they passed away, or in the clinic or in
hospital where they died; thereafter, since in a retrospective manner they have to review the life that they just
finished, it is clear that they will live in those places where
they lived before.

5. How do the deceased ones dress?

Samael Aun Weor: They dress as they were accustomed to dress
in life; in general, they dress in the same clothes in which
they were buried.

6. What type of entertainment do the deceased ones have?

Samael Aun Weor: It is clear that the drunkard will continue to
go to the bars, the movie afficionado to the cinemas, the

gambler to the casinos, the whore to the whorehouse, and the whoremonger to procure them.

7. What sun illuminates the deceased ones?

Samael Aun Weor: The sun that illuminates the dead is the same one that illuminates the living, with the only difference that the deceased ones see the colors beyond the solar spectrum. The dead see colors that are not perceived by the physical retina of mortal people.

8. Do the deceased ones bathe, and if they do, with what water?

Samael Aun Weor: It is obvious that they bathe with the same waters that bathe the living ones, only that they use the water of the fourth dimension.

9. Why do some people die more rapidly than others?

Samael Aun Weor: It is because there are people who stick too much to the physical world, and is clear that they do not want to go away from it, thus they delay, agonizing for hours and hours.

10. What hope do the deceased ones have?

Samael Aun Weor: This topic about hope varies greatly; it depends on the psychological quality of the dead: namely, the greatest hope of an avaricious one—even after dead, since his consciousness is asleep—is to obtain more wealth; the greatest hope of a womanizer will then be to obtain women who will adore him, that will desire him, that will idolize him; the greatest hope of a deeply religious man will be to enter the indescribable regions of the Light, etc.

11. What does the soul look for after it leaves the body?

Samael Aun Weor: The soul looks for what it longs for, namely, the mother looks for her son and sometimes will make herself visible; the husband looks for his wife, if he indeed adored her; and the one who leaves buried treasures will look for them in the place where he left his wealth, etc.

12. Do the deceased ones have authorities as in the physical world?

> Samael Aun Weor: Authorities exist in all the corners of the universe, as much among the living as among the dead. For example, the authorities of the lost souls that live in the abyss will be the demons, whereas the authorities of the ineffable ones will be those that are over them in the scale of their hierarchy. However, since people have their consciousness asleep, it is obvious that they will continue to respect the authorities that exist in the physical world.

13. How do the dead see the world of the living?

> Samael Aun Weor: They see the same streets, the same cities, and the people just as if they were physically alive.

14. Why do the deceased ones not realize that they are dead?

> Samael Aun Weor: The deceased continue to think that they are alive because they have their consciousness asleep, thus, since they see all things absolutely the same as when they were physically alive, it is clear that they do not suspect that they have died, therefore, it is very difficult to make them understand that they no longer belong to the world of the living.

15. To what do the deceased devote themselves?

> Samael Aun Weor: The souls of people who have died—since they do not suspect that they have died—keep themselves occupied in the same ways as when they were physically alive.

16. Can a deceased one transport himself to where he wants, as when he was alive?

> Samael Aun Weor: The deceased have total freedom to move in all the extensions of space and to visit all places.

17. With what light do the deceased illuminate themselves?

> Samael Aun Weor: The deceased illuminate themselves with the astral light; such light is a fire detached from the nimbus of the sun and fixed to the Earth by the force of gravity and the weight of the atmosphere.

18. Does one feel some pain when dying?

Samael Aun Weor: Death is painful for young people and delectable for the elders. This is similar to a fruit: when it is already ripe it falls by his own weight, but when it is unripe it does not easily fall, thus we can state that it suffers because of its release.

19. When already dead, can the dead recognize their corpse in the coffin?

Samael Aun Weor: They can see it, but they do not recognize it because they have their consciousness asleep, thus they never think that such a corpse is their own physical body, and think that it is the body of another person.

20. If the person realizes that he died, could he re-enter the body before it is buried?

Samael Aun Weor: After the thread of life has been cut, it is no longer possible to re-enter the body; in this case, when the person is conscious that he indeed died, he would be either terribly scared or would be glad; everything depends on the moral condition of the deceased.

21. What relief does the soul receive when the body dies?

Samael Aun Weor: The relief of the deceased is the prayer of those who mourn for them; it is essential to pray for the dead.

22. Does one have his hour, day, and minute fixed for his death?

Samael Aun Weor: Every person who comes to this world receives a capital of vital values; death occurs when such capital is exhausted. It is good for us to clarify that we can save such values and therefore extend our life. Those who do not know how to save their vital values die very soon.

23. Can the deceased take the living to the world of dead?

Samael Aun Weor: We Gnostics learn how to willingly leave the physical body, thus, we can visit the world of the dead; also, on some occasions the deceased can take the souls of their friends; specifically, this happens during dreams, but they must return to the physical world when waking from their normal sleep; this means that the visit to the world of the dead is done during the sleep of the body.

24. Are there airplanes, cars, and trains in the world of the deceased as in the physical world?

Samael Aun Weor: Indeed, all the inventions that exist in the physical world come from the region of dead; in their depth, such devices are mental forms that the deceased can see, hear, touch, and feel.

Third Chapter
The Law of Return

1. What is understood by return?

Samael Aun Weor: Common and ordinary people understand by return the return to a new womb; this means that we as souls can reincorporate ourselves within a new human organism. It is not irrelevant to state that when we return we are born and continue to exist in the same manner, in the same way lived by us in our present existence.

2. Why is it that we do not remember anything of our previous lives?

Samael Aun Weor: People do not remember their previous lives because their consciousness is asleep; it is clear that if their consciousness were awakened then they would remember their previous lives.

3. Who returns?

Samael Aun Weor: The souls who still have the possibility of salvation can return to a new womb in order to re-attire themselves again with a new physical body; however when the case is lost, when we have become definitively evil, when already any punishment has no purpose for us, then it is clear that we no longer return, we do not return into a new body anymore, and instead we enter into the infernal worlds where only weeping and gnashing of teeth are heard.

4. How can we verify that we returned to this world anew?

Samael Aun Weor: For some people the return to this world after death is another theory, for others a dogma, a cause for laughter, a superstition, or a belief; but for those who remember our past lives, return is a fact; this means that only by remembering our previous existences will we be able to demonstrate the crude reality of the reincorporation or return to this valley of tears; however, we repeat, to remember our last lives is only possible by the awakening of the consciousness.

5. Why do we come to this world again?

Samael Aun Weor: We return to this world with the purpose of becoming perfect, because unfortunately we are sinners and we need to end with our errors.

6. What returns to the world of human beings?

Samael Aun Weor: What returns to this world is the soul of the deceased.

7. Do animals and plants also return to this world?

Samael Aun Weor: The souls of plants, animals, and stones are the elementals of nature; they also return to this world in continuous manner. For example, if a plant dries up and dies, then the elemental of such a plant is reborn again in a new plant; if an animal dies, the elemental of that creature returns in a new animal organism again, etc.

8. Does predestination exist?

Samael Aun Weor: Each soul is the creator of its own destiny; if one performs good deeds, one then receives good luck, however if one performs evil deeds, then one is reborn in this world in order suffer and to pay everything; now we can understand why some are born on mattresses filled with white goose feathers and others in disgrace.

9. I would like to remember my past lives, but since I have my consciousness asleep, how can I awaken it?

Samael Aun Weor: Follow the path of the sanctity; that is the way for the awakening of the consciousness. Terminate with all of your errors, repent of all of your evil deeds, become pure in thought, word, and action; I guarantee you that your consciousness will totally awaken when you have reached true sanctity.

10. Why do many of us not believe that we have had previous lives?

Samael Aun Weor: Some people do not believe that they had previous lives simply because they do not remember them, and indeed they do not remember them because their consciousness is totally asleep.

11. Sir, do you remember your previous lives? Is it verifiable to you that reincorporation exists?

Samael Aun Weor: It is clear that if I did not remember my previous lives, I would not dare to defend the doctrine of return with so much passion; fortunately, I remember with entire exactitude all the lives that I have had on the planet Earth.

12. How many times can one return?

Samael Aun Weor: It is written with golden letters in the book of life that one returns to this world 108 times.

13. Why do some souls return as men and others as women?

Samael Aun Weor: Everything depends on the events of life; sometimes we must return in feminine body and others in masculine; this is according to the events of our previous lives.

14. Why do some say that if one treats animals badly one can return as a horse, dog, or cat, etc.?

Samael Aun Weor: The lost souls enter the infernal worlds; there, as it is stated in the sacred scriptures, they suffer the Second Death; it is after such a death that the condemned souls become free of any sin; then they can return to this world. However, they return according to the law of evolution, namely, they evolve, returning as mineral elementals; thereafter they ascend to the plant state, then later the souls reincorporate within animal organisms, and finally reconquer the human state that once they lost. When arriving at these heights, 108 lives are assigned to them again, so that they can become perfect; nevertheless, if they fail again, then the same process is repeated anew.

15. How is it that when one visits certain places one has the sensation of knowing the place so well that one can even give details and signs of the same place?

Samael Aun Weor: That phenomenon happens because in previous lives we were in that place.

16. How many opportunities does one have in order to return
as a human being, how many as an animal, how many as a
plant, and how many as a mineral?

Samael Aun Weor: The return in human organisms is already
properly calculated as 108 times. But the return in plant
or animals organisms, or simply as mineral elementals,
does not have an exact number.

17. Is it possible to pass from the plant kingdom to the human
kingdom or from the animal to the mineral?

Samael Aun Weor: From the plant kingdom one passes into the
human kingdom—but through the animal kingdom; this
means that we cannot skip a step, because "nature does
not make leaps." If animal elementals degenerate, then
they devolve; they go back down to the mineral state but
first by passing—naturally—through the plant state.

18. In what dimension are the elementals from plants and
minerals located?

Samael Aun Weor: The elemental creatures of nature live in the
fourth dimension.

19. Are we the same human souls from ancient times, those
who return, or do some definitively disappear?

Samael Aun Weor: The present humanity is very old; it has
been returning to this world for million of years.

20. How long does it take for a human soul—after physically
dying—to receive a new body?

Samael Aun Weor: That depends upon the destiny of each one;
some are reborn again immediately and others delay a
long time in order to return.

21. As to students who have begun to awaken their consciousness: when they die, can they be aware of the return process?

Samael Aun Weor: Whosoever awakens the consciousness does
not need to wait for the moment of the death in order to
remember their previous lives; they can remember them in
life, here and now.

22. Does Gnosis consider unfair the fact that millions of human beings live in the most complete ignorance about their evolution, return, the inner realization of their Being, and the awakening of their consciousness?

Samael Aun Weor: We Gnostics consider unfair the fact that there are not enough instructors, or better said, a great quantity of missionaries to deliver the Gnostic teachings everywhere. Nevertheless, we are not guilty of this, since this humanity is only interested in amusing themselves, obtaining money, giving themselves to pleasures, etc. If people were more comprehensive, they would be more concerned with these studies and would spread them.

23. What is the Second Death and what does it have to do with return?

Samael Aun Weor: The Second Death is the termination of our animal passions in the infernal worlds; this means that through its fulfillment the condemned—the lost ones— arrive at the original purity, and when this happens they leave the infernal abysses, which exist within the interior of the Earth. Then, as we already stated, such souls evolve again from stone to man.

24. When will it be possible for humanity to understand "the why" of returning?

Samael Aun Weor: Humanity will only be able to understand "the why" of returning when they attain the awakening of their consciousness.

25. Why is it that people are born, die, and return again just to repeat the same song?

Samael Aun Weor: Certainly, people—as you stated—are born and die and return again in order to repeat the same song because we are submitted to the Law of Recurrence. In each life, we return in order to repeat everything which we did in the previous life, but we suffer the consequences of the good and bad things we did in the last life; this is a vicious circle, a repetition of dramas, scenes, loves, encounters with the same people, etc.

26. What should we do in order to cease so many repetitions?

    Samael Aun Weor: Only by means of sanctification is it possible for us to get rid of the Law of Recurrence.

27. Who send us to take a physical body again?

    Samael Aun Weor: The Angels of Destiny send us to this world; they have written down in their books our good and bad actions.

28. If after the death of the physical body, the soul goes to heaven—as it is stated by many religions—why does it not stay there?

    Samael Aun Weor: Heaven is a reward and a recompense for our good actions. However, when the recompense is exhausted, it is then clear that we must return to this world.

29. Is it true that hell exists?

    Samael Aun Weor: That hell with flames—that pit with ignited coals and devils with forks—is a symbol that corresponds to a tremendous reality; in other worlds, the infernal worlds, the inferior worlds, are regions of bitterness within the interior of the planet Earth; the lost souls live in those infradimensional abysses.

30. If some souls go to hell, what can we do in order to avoid falling into those flames?

    Samael Aun Weor: To teach the Gnostic doctrine to all souls is our duty, since it would be unjust—as we already stated in a previous answer—to not preach these teachings in all the regions of the world.

31. Is it true that the souls fall into that pit full of flames and yet are not burned?

    Samael Aun Weor: Within the interior of the Earth exists the fire and the water; the failed souls become identified with these elements of nature and suffer. However, the fire cannot burn them nor the water drown them, because the souls are incorporeal, subtle. When seeing this subject-matter about the flames from another angle, I want tell you that such flames symbolize our animal passions.

32. Who saw those flames and became aware that the souls were there?

Samael Aun Weor: Any intelligent person knows that liquid fire exists within the interior of the Earth, since volcanoes show it; so, it is not necessary to be wise in order to see the flames; anyone can see those flames within volcanoes' craters, mixed with lava and flammable gases.

33. What is the Purgatorial region?

Samael Aun Weor: Religions address us about Purgatory, about the Purgatorial region; in fact, there exist inferior and submerged molecular zones located beyond the fourth dimension. In such zones, many souls that aspire to the Light are purified by eliminating their sins.

34. Is it true that by believing in God one can escape hell?

Samael Aun Weor: Many people believe in God and, nevertheless, they do not escape hell; if you want to escape from falling into the region of the darkness, then you need to sanctify yourself.

35. Is it true that by learning by memory the chapters of the Bible one can be free of hell?

Samael Aun Weor: Many people who know the Bible by memory—with periods and commas—abide in hell.

36. Could somebody be saved just by believing what is written in the Bible?

Samael Aun Weor: Faith without works is dead faith; we need living faith, and this is based on good works. It is urgent to live in accordance with the teachings of our Lord Jesus Christ.

37. Is returning an obligation?

Samael Aun Weor: As long as we do not attain perfection, the Angels of Destiny will send us to this world.

38. Is returning favorable in order to pay for our bad deeds?

Samael Aun Weor: All the sufferings that we have in this world are due to the bad actions from our previous lives.

39. Do we always return in the same family?

Samael Aun Weor: The "I" continues in its own seed; this means that we continue in our descendants. In other words, we return to the same family.

40. What is the difference between return and reincarnation?

Samael Aun Weor: The egos "**return** incessantly" in order to repeat dramas, scenes, events, here and now. The ego returns in order to pay Karma and to satisfy its desires.

The word **reincarnation** is very demanding. Nobody could reincarnate without previously having eliminated the ego. It would be absurd to confuse reincarnation with return. The humanoids return with their consciousness asleep, whereas Masters like Jesus, Buddha, Krishna, etc., reincarnate by will.

Fourth Chapter

The Law of Karma

1. What answer can be given to the profane ones who—when speaking to them about the law of return—allege that they cannot believe in it, since nobody has gone and returned in order to narrate what they have seen?

Samael Aun Weor: Days come and go; the suns return to their point of departure after thousands of years; the years return time and time again; the four stations of spring, summer, autumn, and winter always return: so, there is no need to believe in the law of return since it is so evident, given that everybody is seeing it every day. Thus also the souls return, come again to this world, since "return" is a law that exists in all creation.

2. How can we demonstrate the existence of the law of return?

Samael Aun Weor: By awakening the consciousness we can all demonstrate the law of the eternal return. We Gnostics have systems, methods, in order to awaken the consciousness; thus, the person who is awakened can remember their past lives. Therefore, to those who remember their past lives, the law of the eternal return is a fact.

3. Why there are some people who are well educated, who work and who fight a lot in order to achieve status yet they do not achieve it, yet others with less preparation and without efforts achieve the wished success?

Samael Aun Weor: Everything depends on the law of Karma. This word (Karma) means "action and consequence." If in past lives we have done much good, then in the present life we triumph with happiness; but if in recent lives we have done much bad, then we fail in our present life.

4. Why are there families who—no matter how hard they try—do not manage to have friends anywhere, yet for others it is so easy to have friends wherever they go?

Samael Aun Weor: In previous lives we have had many friends and enemies; when returning or coming back to this world, we again encounter those friends and those enemies, then everything is repeated as it happened in the past; nevertheless, there are also some difficult people that do not like to have friends—misanthropists we would call them—these are people who hide themselves, who move away, who separate themselves from society, solitary by nature and by instinct. When such people return to this world, they usually find themselves alone; nobody gets along with them. However, there are other people who in past lives knew how to fulfill their duties with society, with the world, and they even worked on behalf of their fellowmen; thus, it is logical that when they return to this world they are surrounded by those souls who in ancient times or past lives formed their social circle, and therefore they enjoy—as is natural—much affection.

5. What is the cause when some housewives—although they treat their servants very well—never find maids who help them faithfully, while for other housewives all maids are faithful?

Samael Aun Weor: Those housewives who do not find faithful and sincere maids were in previous lives tyrannical and cruel with their servants. Now they do not find maids who can really serve them because in the past they never knew how to serve; thus, this is the consequence.

6. Why there are people who from their birth until their death work without rest as if they were undergoing a sentence, while there are others who live very well without so much work?

Samael Aun Weor: That is because of the Law of Karma. In past lives, people who work excessively and do not progress made others work very much, and exploited their employees in a pitiless manner; thus, now they undergo the consequences by working uselessly, since they do not progress.

7. My son married and his marriage became extremely bad, all the businesses where he worked went bankrupt; he asked for a loan from the bank in order to open a small business and he failed completely. Everything that he undertook failed; he had to divorce his wife because of the many misfortunes that they had. After some time he married again, and that man—for whom only begging for alms remained—now is very well and his success increases every day. What it is the cause of this?

Samael Aun Weor: There exist three types of marriage bonds: first, Karmic; second, Dharmic; and third, Cosmic.

The first type consists of pain, misery, hunger, nakedness, disgrace; the second consists of success, happiness, love, economic progress, etc.; and the third is only for the chosen souls, pure, holy: the third brings, as it is natural, inexhaustible happiness.

Therefore, regarding the case that you ask about, we must tell you that amongst these three married states it belongs to the first order (Karmic). There is no doubt that your son and his first wife underwent the unspeakable in order to pay for the bad actions of their previous lives; it is clear that they were also husband and wife in past lives, and that they did much bad; they did not know how to live, therefore the outcome was pain. The new marriage of your son is benign from the economic point of view; we can qualify it as a marriage of good luck, better said, Dharmic, the outcome of good deeds from previous lives; the second wife also lived with him in past lives and since with her he observed better conduct, the outcome is that now luck changed for him, improved his life, and that is all.

8. My son has been sick for five years. We have spent a lot of money on doctors yet they have not found the exact cause of his sickness; some say that perhaps it is because of a nervous shock, since he was quite an intelligent boy in his

studies; others suppose that he has been a victim of works of witchcraft; what is your opinion?

Samael Aun Weor: Obviously, by all means and under the light of dazzling clarity, we see a punishment, a mental Karma because of an erroneous use of the mind in previous lives. Now, if you want your son to become healed, then, first struggle for the healing of other mental patients, in order to modify the original cause. Remember that the effect is modified only by modifying the cause. Unfortunately, patients have the marked tendency of locking themselves within their own circle; very seldom in life do we see the case of a patient who worries for the healing of other patients; yet, if somebody does so, it is clear that he will also heal himself of his own pains; therefore, we advise you—since in this precise case your son cannot dedicate himself to the healing of others—do it in name of your son. Do not forget works of charity; be concerned for the health of all those mental patients that cross your way: perform good by the ton. Do not forget either that in the invisible world exist very wise Masters who can help you in this concrete case of your son; I want now to talk in a specific manner about to glorious Angel Adonai, the Angel of Light and Joy; such a Master is very wise, and if you concentrate yourself intensely on him, begging him in name of Christ to heal your son, I am completely sure that in no way would he refuse to make this work of charity for you. Nevertheless, do not forget to "Strike with thy rod while thou beg to thy God"—beseech and perform good by the ton; that is the way.

9. I had the opportunity of witnessing the case of a marriage in Santa Marta, Colombia. They had a very good business, but from one moment to another it was burned; thereafter the gentleman became ill and died of tuberculosis; twenty years later I found that his wife was close to death, also from tuberculosis. What would be the cause of this?

Samael Aun Weor: It is good for you to know that tuberculosis is due to the lack of religion, to materialism, to life without devotion and love for God in previous lives; therefore, this is the cause for that gentleman to die of tuberculosis, and if he lost his goods, it is clear that he ended with the goods of other people in his previous life. He burned other people's goods and therefore they burned his goods; he damaged others, and therefore they damaged him; this is called Karma, punishment. Tuberculosis did not entirely affect his wife because in her previous lives the lack of religiosity was not so absolutely crude; to some extent she must have had some spirituality.

10. I have a very good son who worked and gave everything that he gained to me, but then he fell in love with an older lady, a friend of mine who has three children from a married man; he joined her in order to live together without legally marrying her. Thereafter, even when he worked, money did not come to him, even to the point that he came to me demanding an amount of money, alleging that he was going to undertake a business (something that he never did). As soon as they finished with the money that I gave him, the lady left him. Now he lives alone; he works, but is totally ruined. What is the cause of this?

Samael Aun Weor: Adultery sticks out—at first glance—with all its painful consequences: loss of money, bad situations, intense moral sufferings, etc., which are the outcome of error.

11. I want you to tell me if his situation could improve?

Samael Aun Weor: If on one of the plates of the cosmic scale we place the good actions and in the other the bad ones and if the latter weighs more, it is clear that the scale will incline against us, producing bitterness for us. But if we put good deeds on the plate of good, then we can incline the scale in our favor; then our luck will improve remarkably. Therefore, if that son of yours dedicates himself to performing good deeds, his luck will improve.

12. I have a twenty year old son, who since two years ago does not want to live at home, but at my friends' house. He does not want to study nor to work; he comes for a month to

my house, he feels happy for a while, and later he becomes angry with everybody and again leaves the house. I am hoping you can tell me the cause of this.

Samael Aun Weor: That son of yours has only created problems for you. It is clear that the outcome of disorder will be pain. There is no doubt that he does not know nor does he want to learn how to live; however, it is necessary to take care of him as best is possible, with infinite patience and love. There is no doubt that in the future he will have big problems with bitter consequences. Then he will begin to comprehend the necessity of establishing order in his life.

Fifth Chapter
Ghosts

1. Have you ever seen a ghost?

Samael Aun Weor: Some people believe in ghosts, others doubt, and finally there are others who make a derision of them. I do not need to believe, doubt, or laugh about them, since for me the existence of ghosts is a fact.

2. Have you confirmed the existence of ghosts? Have you seen them?

Samael Aun Weor: Friend, it is not irrelevant to narrate a very interesting case to you. She was still very young and her name was Angela; indeed, she was quite an extraordinary girlfriend, although today she is already dead. One day, while she was still alive, I decided to move away from her without any notice. I went towards the coasts of the Atlantic Ocean and accommodated myself in the house of an elderly lady, a noble woman who did not deny me her hospitality. I made my room within the living room of the house, whose door went directly to the street. My bed was a tropical canvas camp bed and since there were a lot of mosquitoes, I protected myself with a very fine and transparent net.

One night while laying on my bed and dozing, unexpectedly someone knocked rhythmically three times at my door. At the moment in which I sat up in order to rise and go towards the door, I felt a pair of hands penetrate through my fine and transparent net; ominously, the hands approached me and caressed my face. However this ominous experience did not finish there, since in addition to those hands, a human ghost appeared with the semblance of that girlfriend—who, frankly, did not attract me. The distressed phantom wept while telling me the following phrases: "Ungrateful, you moved away without saying farewell to me; how much I loved and adored you with all of my heart," etc., and other things.

I wanted to speak, but everything was useless because my tongue was tied; then mentally, I ordered to that ghost to withdraw immediately.

However, the phantom uttered new moans and new recriminations; then the phantom said, "Okay, I am going away," and slowly, slowly moved away. Then, when I saw that the apparition was leaving, a new thought, a special idea, arose within my mind. I said to myself: "This is the moment to find out what a ghost is, what it is made of, what of it is real."

It is obvious that when I started thinking in this way, fear disappeared from me and my tongue was loosened; then I could speak. Thus, I command the ghost: "Do not go away, come back, I need to talk to you."

The ghost then answered, "Okay I am coming. I will not leave then." It is not irrelevant to state that such words were associated with actions, so that ghost came again towards me.

What I did first was to examine my own faculties in order to check if they were working correctly. Then I said to myself, "I am not drunk, nor I am hypnotized. I am not a victim of any hallucination, since my five senses are working correctly, thus I do not have reason to doubt."

So, having verified the proper functioning of my five senses, I came then to examine the ghost as follow: "Give me your hand," I said to the apparition; it is obvious that the phantom did not refuse my demands thus she extended her right hand to me. I held the arm of that extraordinary figure that was in front of me and I noticed a normal rhythmical march as if it had a heart. I auscultated the liver, spleen, etc. thus, every organ in it functioned correctly; however the quality of that matter seemed rather like a protoplasm, a gelatinous substance, similar—when touching it—to vinyl; I performed such an examination under the light of a bulb properly lit; the examination lasted about half an hour.

Later, I dismissed the ghost by telling her, "Now you can leave. I am satisfied with the examination." While uttering multiple recriminations, the ghost withdrew, crying bitterly.

Moments later, the owner of the house knocked at the door; she thought that I had just disrespected the hospitality of her house; she entered and said to me that she had given hospitality only to me, and that she was surprised that I was bringing women into the room.

"My apologies to you, dear lady," was my answer, "but I have not brought any woman here, a ghost has visited me, and that is all." (It is clear that I narrated the whole incident to her). The lady was convinced, since she shook terribly when perceiving a frightful cold in the midst of the room—in completely tropical weather—which confirmed to her the veracity of my narration.

I wrote down the day, date, and hour of the event, and later on when I encountered that girlfriend I narrated my experience to her. She told me that on that night and at that hour mentioned by me, she was sleeping and dreaming that she was in a coastal place talking to me within a room similar to a living room.

I said to myself, "It is obvious that this woman went to sleep thinking of me, and this is why her ghost visited me."

The peculiar aspect of this is that several months later that woman died, and one night while I was resting in my bed, the phenomenon was repeated, but this time the ghost—full of tenderness and affection—intended to lie down next to me. Since this matter was becoming quite horrific, I had no alternative but to command the phantom in a very severe manner to leave me forever and to not ever bother me in life; thus, the ghost did it as commanded and it never returned again.

3. Your narration was very intriguing, sir; would you please
narrate another similar case to us?

Samael Aun Weor: With pleasure, my friend: on a certain
occasion a poor young woman arrived at the city. She
was in a terrible economic situation; she was an honest
girl and asked to work for me. Thus, I did not have any
inconvenience in employing her as a maid in my house;
she turned out to be a very diligent worker. Unfortunately,
a few days after she started working in my house, a series
of extraordinary psychic phenomena happened that not
only disturbed my relatives, but also the people of my
neighborhood.

Before her presence the dishware rose in the air and
crashed against the floor into fragments; likewise, the
tables, the chairs, were dancing by themselves, and stones
were falling within our home. It was not very pleasant
for us that at the precise moments of eating at the table,
stones, dirt, etc., etc. were falling into our food.

This young girl had on her right hand a mysterious ring
with an inscription that said exactly the following: "A
reminder of your friend Luzbel."

What is most intriguing is that although that woman was
in misfortune (economically speaking) she did not stop
receiving coins—which she always spent in order to eat—
from her mentioned friend; such money came through
the air and she simply gathered it.

The girl told us that her "friend" told her that he lived in
the sea and that he wanted to take her to the bottom of
the ocean.

Many times we performed conjurations in order to push
away her invisible comrade, but he always returned with
more force, and returned to his devious actions, and the
people, as is natural, were always alarmed.

Some young men fell in love with her, but when they tried
to approach their lady, stones rained on them; thus, they
fled terrified and horrified.

Later, this girl moved away from the neighborhoods of the city; what became of her? We do not know. However, what indeed we could verify is that "Luzbel"—her peculiar friend—was simply an elemental of the ocean. There is no doubt that she had much of an elemental nature; this is what her eyes, her glance, her body, her way of being, etc., showed to us.

APOLLO 13

A potential disaster turned into NASA's "successful failure" in April of 1970, when the crew of Apollo 13 used the Lunar Module as a lifeboat to return to Earth. An explosion in the craft's oxygen tanks had crippled the Command Module, preventing a landing on the Moon. [Quoted from Nasa]

Sixth Chapter
Human Karmic Instances

1. I am going to narrate to you a case that happened to me
some time ago. We moved out of the house in which we had
lived for eleven years and where we had a lot of bad luck.
Since some of our belongings had been left behind, my aunt
and I went back to that house a few days later. Immediately
upon entering we smelled the foul stench of a corpse; since
we had left the house totally clean, I was curious, so I went
to the second floor in order to inspect it. When entering
one of the bedrooms, I saw—in the place formerly occupied
by one of the beds—a deep hole, as if someone was going to
place a coffin in it. I uttered a shout, and my aunt came up
when hearing it; then, because she saw that I was so frightened, we left that house immediately and went back to the
house where we live now.

From that moment, I began to lose my appetite. I was
scarcely eating, little by little, until the moment in which I
could not eat any type of food. In two months I lost forty
pounds, therefore, they had to place me in a sanatorium.
Many specialists examined me; yet, no one could find the
cause of my problem. I was dying and suffering a pain in
my stomach which did not stop not even for a minute—
medicines, meals, I could not ingest anything; everything
had to be injected.

After eight days as a patient in the sanatorium, I entered
into a comatose state. The physicians exhausted all efforts
trying heal me, and their diagnosis was cancer, since indeed
my body was exhaling the scent of a cancerous body. They
wanted to perform surgery on me but my relatives did not
allow it.

I always saw next to me a doctor with a long white robe; he
was unknown to me and my relatives, because he was not
assisting me in this physical world. That doctor—who was
invisible to all except to me—comforted me and promised to

heal me. Certainly his word was fulfilled, and I was miracu-
lously cured. So, when the surgeons finally operated upon
me in order to discover the *cause causarum* of my disease,
with astonishment they discovered that I was totally healed;
the supposed cancer did not exist.

Could you tell me what happened? What was the cause of
my disease? This has always been an enigma for me.

Samael Aun Weor: With great pleasure I will answer your
question. Allow me to tell you dear young lady that in
your past existence—which indeed you had here in the
capital city of Mexico—you committed an act of black
magic against another person that produced his death;
thus, your mysterious disease was the outcome of that. If
you were healed, if you did not die, it is because in your
present life you have done good actions which allowed the
diminishing your Karma. You were indeed attended by an
invisible doctor; therefore, you must be immensely thankful for it.

2. We were three siblings from the first marriage of my father,
whose relatives took my older brother away from my mother
when he became one year old; then, when I was five years
old, my mother gave me away to my father, who lived with
his mother and my older brother.

During all of my childhood, I never received affection from
any of them because of the hatred that my grandma always
had against me, so they did not care about me in order to
not upset her. I never knew if my mother was alive until I
was fifteen years old; my mother was the only one who gave
me affection until her death ten years ago.

I would like to know why I have not been able to find happiness and the love of a man, and what was the cause of the
great hatred on the part of my grandmother?

Samael Aun Weor: Turn around the videotape of your story
and you will have the answer, since it is obvious that all of
those events of your life are a repetition of your previous
existence, where you—instead of being the prey—were the
predator. Those who today have provided you with so

much pain were your victims in the past, and that is all. Remember that the Law of Karma is the faithful balance of all our actions; there can be no effect without a cause, nor cause without effect. Therefore, you have collected the consequences of your own acts. If you were to remember your previous life or your previous lives, then you could verify the reality of my words.

3. Could you explain why I cannot find love in my life in spite of longing so much for it?

Samael Aun Weor: Based on the law of action and consequence, we always harvest what we sow; thus, by logical consequence we can see that since you sowed storms, you harvested lightning.

4. Would you narrate for us some concrete case of a disease the cause of which is based in bad actions from previous lives?

Samael Aun Weor: With greatest pleasure. In my last reincarnation I knew the case of a bandit who was shot; his execution happened on a road. This bandit was called by the nickname "Golondrino" (wanderer). He fell into the hands of justice, was tied to a tree, and received the death sentence.

Much later, that man was reborn into a feminine body. So, one day her relatives asked me for help. This young and very distinguished lady—within which the soul of the "Wanderer" had reincorporated—was foaming at the mouth and her body was writhing horribly while shouting, full of terror, the following phrases: "The police are already coming for me, they say that I am a thief, a road bandit, they have tied me to this tree and they are going to shoot me." The last words were always accompanied by movements of her hands making effort as if she wanted to untie invisible bows, strange cords.

Our investigations revealed to us this concrete case; it was therefore related to a mental repetition of the final episode of the previous life of the soul incarnated in the woman's body.

Psychiatrists totally failed; they could not heal her. We had to appeal to certain magical conjurations; thus, the outcome was astounding, since the patient was radically healed. There is no doubt that we were assisted by the divine power of the Holy Spirit.

5. We lived in a house with the number thirteen on the door and we were thirteen in our family; during the eleven years we were in that house there was nothing but disease and misery. Could you tell us what is the cause of this?

Samael Aun Weor: Respectable young lady, I will answer your question with pleasure. Remember that the mission of the cosmic ship Apollo 13 was a complete failure; the plan of the United States for the conquest of space by had to be postponed since the three astronauts of the crew were on the verge of perishing.

At these moments, the memory of one New Year's Eve comes to my memory. We, thirteen people, were reunited around a table; in the midst of that banquet I said to the guests, "One from among us, the thirteen people that are here reunited, will soon die." Such a prophecy was fulfilled some months later, when one of those guests passed away.

Do not become surprised then by the fatidic thirteen; such a number is death, fatality, tragedy, pain; nevertheless, the thirteen also brings new situations, since death and life are found intimately related; it is clear that you were paying a frightful Karma. That is all.

6. Could you tell me why I have always failed with love? When I am on the verge of reaching happiness, it flies away from my hand. Even when they always say that they love me, they run away from me to marry another woman.

Samael Aun Weor: Respectable lady, with great pleasure I will answer your question. It is clear that your problem could not in any way be properly understood if we ignored the law of the eternal return. Listen: all events are an incessant repetition of the events of different past lives. Every human being has contracted diverse marriages in past lives, or has settled down into sexual relations with other people, etc., thus, the outcome of such conjugal associations can be good, bad, or indifferent. If we have behaved badly with a determined spouse, then in a new life the re-encounter with its consequences are settled down: failed marriages, frustrations of weddings, the rupture of loving relations, etc. What is the most serious of all this is the legal separation forced by such-and-such reason, and mainly when there is love.

"If ye have faith as a grain of mustard seed, ye shall say unto this mountain, Remove hence to yonder place; and it shall remove; and nothing shall be impossible unto you." – Matthew 17:20

Seventh Chapter

Intriguing Narrations

1. One night in April 1968, while I was profoundly asleep, I heard shouts and noises as if from people breaking glass and fighting in the street. Fearing that eventually they could break the glass of my car which was parked in the street, I got up, took my slippers and pants, and went through the corridor. I crossed the room and, raising the curtain, looked through the window and discovered with surprise that there were no people there, no noises; instead, there was peace and tranquility. The street was totally illuminated and my car in a perfect state. Thinking that everything was just the outcome of an illusion or nightmare, I walked back again through the corridor to the door of my bedroom; thus, when I opened the door and walked a few steps, I was astounded when seeing myself profoundly asleep in the bed and next to my wife. I was with my arms out and on the blankets, the left leg totally uncovered, and my face resting on its left side. When seeing this scene, a great terror entered me; then I felt myself being attracted towards my body as if it was a strong magnet; then I woke up very frightened with strong beats of my heart and a cold sweat over all of my body. Can you tell me what actually happened?

    Samael Aun Weor: This is a concrete case of what is called an astral projection; your soul became detached from your physical body. It is clear that during common, ordinary, normal sleep, every soul leaves the body and wanders around; it goes to different places. Thereafter, it returns to its physical body at the precise moment of waking up; indeed, the vigil state starts when the soul again enters its body of bones and flesh.

    The intriguing aspect of your case is that when you as soul went back to your bedroom, you could see your physical body sleeping in the bed; you saw it in the same manner as when you can see a table or a car in order to drive it.

Likewise, you as a soul entered in the body, woke up, and came to the vigil state; so this is what happened to you.

2. In the year 1958, when I went back to my home after watching a movie in a cinema, I found my family very preoccupied because of the disappearance of an aunt who had gone out to the street, leaving alone in the house her children (four, from 3 to 6 years old), who were crying from fear and hunger. My relatives had gone to several places to look for her, yet everything had been useless; they were organizing themselves in order to go, look, and ask for her everywhere; they decided that I must remain in the house.

About three o'clock in the morning, alarmed, I woke up and saw the room was totally dark; then, all of a sudden, in the center of the room an oval shaped figure began to be illuminated. It came to my bed, arrived at the edge of it, and raised the mosquito net. On the edge of my bed I felt something like a body sit, which then totally took the figure of my aunt who they were looking for. She told me in a loud voice the following: "Dear one of mine, do not be scared. I am your aunt. I have just come to tell you that I am already dead, and I want you to tell them where they can find my corpse. Locate your uncle and tell him that they must look for me at police station 'x.' I very much request from you to take care and pray for my children." Thereafter, she got up, lowered the mosquito net, and disappeared.

The following day I did what she told me to do, yet nobody believed me until they were convinced that indeed the deformed corpse of my aunt (because she died within a steam bath) was in that police station.

How is it possible that after having died a person can give data for the location of her corpse and request care for her children?

Samael Aun Weor: After the death of the physical body, the soul lives in the superior dimensions of nature and the cosmos; we already stated this in a previous chapter, but it is not irrelevant to repeat it. It is clear that such a soul needed to inform you about the death of her body; that report was necessary, since she had children and she had to fulfill her duties. Undoubtedly, in this case that soul was assisted by the superior laws, which allowed her to enter into the tridimensional world in which we live in order to give you complete information about the location of her corpse—a fact that was properly verified, since the body was found exactly in the place where she said that it was, that is, in a police station; so facts are facts, and before the facts we must surrender.

3. Once when I was at a Gnostic meeting, a person approached me and requested that I pray for the health of her mother, who was practically hopeless; thus, I promised her that I would do whatever I could for her mother's healing.

Later, I beseeched the Angel Adonai for his assistance; thus, I imagined that I was at the house of the lady—a lovely, elderly lady who I found laid down on her bed and who when seeing me gladly smiled. She sat upright and I put my right hand on her forehead and my left touching her heart; likewise, I strongly concentrated on the Master Jesus for him to help me; I saw how she recovered, and smiling, accompanied me to the door of her house.

In the following meeting, the person who had requested the aid, almost with tears in her eyes, came to thank me and to tell me that her mother had recovered and sent me greetings because she had seen me.

How it is possible that two people solely by faith have obtained an almost miraculous treatment?

Samael Aun Weor: My friend, faith performs miracles. This is why the Divine Master Jesus said: "If ye have faith as a grain of mustard seed, ye shall say unto this mountain, Remove hence to yonder place; and it shall remove; and nothing shall be impossible unto you." - Matthew 17:20

It is clear that when you imagined in a vivid manner being next to the bed of the patient, a projection of your psyche took place; your soul traveled towards the patient and healed the patient with the aid of the Divine Master. Do not be surprised that she has seen you, since when the

"Jesus put his hand on the possessed people and
commanded that the demons leave the body of
the possessed, and it is clear that they obeyed."

soul is projected this is often made visible, even at remote distances. Have you not hear of saints who did the same thing, who during prayer and in a state of ecstasy were seen in other places healing the ill?

4. In another meeting in which we were performing spiritual healing, a lady who was approximately sixty years old arrived. She had very deep knife wounds on her arms—wounds that she showed to all the assistants; after we repeated the words of the conjuration that the Master pronounced, he ask her to sit.

In the following meeting, she showed us her arms again. We then saw that the wounds were almost healed; then we repeated the same procedure, and upon the third meeting she once again showed us her arms. Then, with surprise we saw that where once there was only open flesh, not even a scar of the wound could be found.

What happened in order for this person to heal so perfectly and quickly?

Samael Aun Weor: Ah! Now I understand that you are talking about Gnostic meetings. Certainly, those meetings are very interesting; remember that the primitive Christians were Gnostics who performed wonderful treatments. Therefore, do not be surprised that in those meetings, under the guidance of a Master who instructs such a congregation, another similar miracle has been performed. Gnostics invoke the Divine Beings who live in the invisible world so that they can perform these types of treatments. Thus, there is no doubt that this is what happened and this is why the patient was radically healed.

5. Around the year 1962, approximately the month of November, days in which I had scarcely begun to attend the Gnostic lectures, a gentleman of rare aspect—whose face reflected preoccupation and who had a vague and mysterious glance—presented himself; he requested help in order to remove from his body some "tenebrous entities," which were

hurting him and producing a swelling in his legs, which he showed to us.

The Master acceded and pronounced "The Conjuration of the Seven." He performed some magnetic passes upon him, then the individual began to twist, shout, howl, and complain as if feeling immense pain; at the same time, he was performing gesticulations and movements as if some ominous thing was coming out of him; thereafter, a strong nauseous scent began to permeate the environment. Then there was a pause in which it seemed to have rested; the Master then clapped his hands three times and the man got up, saying that he did not remember anything. In three sessions his legs became perfectly well and he did not complain about the ominous entities anymore. Could you explain what happened, and how this treatment was possible?

Samael Aun Weor: These are cases of possessed people that the Christian Gospel refers to: Jesus put his hand on the possessed people and commanded that the demons leave the body of the possessed, and it is clear that they obeyed.

The Apostles also received such power; Jesus granted such authority to them. This is how they could exorcise the demons and throw them out of the bodies of the patients so that they could be healed. Therefore, the case that you tell me is not a unique case; diseases are produced precisely by tenebrous entities that introduce themselves within the body of the ill.

Many native tribes of America know these mysteries; I know cases of many native priests who exorcise their patients before healing them; this they do with the sane purpose of eliminating the "tenebrous entities" that cause the disease. If our physicians would follow the example of these native healers, it is obvious that they would make wonders in the field of medicine. So, the concrete case that you mention is hardly abnormal; the patient was exorcised and was healed, and that is all.

Do not forget that Rue and Sage smudges can be used in the exorcisms; these are two wonderful plants.

Eighth Chapter

Astral Projection

1. What is an Astral Projection?

Samael Aun Weor: Do you really not know what an Astral Projection is? Young lady, I understand very well that your question is sincere. Listen: Astral Projection is an extremely simple and easy natural phenomenon like eating and drinking, etc. It is clear that when the physical body enters into sleep, the soul leaves it and travels everywhere. When returning, when re-entering into its body again, the soul then often remembers the places where it was, the people with whom it spoke, etc.; usually people describe this phenomenon as dreams, yet indeed this is an astral projection.

2. Can this phenomenon be performed only in dreams or can it also be done by will?

Samael Aun Weor: In either case, the slumber state is necessary in order for one to be able to astral project, even by will.

3. Is Astral Projection dangerous?

Samael Aun Weor: It seems to me that to become cognizant of one's own natural phenomena can never be dangerous. One must become cognizant of the food that one eats, of what one drinks, of the state of one's health, and also of the process of astral projection that occurs in any living creature.

4. Please explain to me the technique to astral project. I would like to go to Paris by will.

Samael Aun Weor: What you always perform in an involuntary and unconscious manner, learn to do in a voluntary and conscious manner. You have always astral projected yourself, since all souls leave the body—unfortunately in an unconscious manner—at the moment when one is dozing; so, perform the same thing, but in a voluntary and conscious manner. I repeat: when you began to feel

that state of lassitude related to slumber, when you begin
to doze, then imagine yourself to be like a subtle and
vaporous ghost; think that you are going to leave your
body; understand that you are not the body; understand
that you are a soul; thus, feel yourself as being soul and
then with smoothness and delicacy—as the souls rise—get
up from your bed. What I am explaining to you must be
performed in a concrete manner; this is not to a matter
of thinking, but of actions! Then as soon you get up,
perform a small jump within your bedroom with the firm
intention of floating in the environment; thus, it is clear
that if you float, it is because you are already outside your
physical body; then you can leave your bedroom and float
in the atmosphere; then you can go to Paris, London, or
wherever pleases you. However, if you do not float it is
because you just got up from your bed with your physical
body; if this happens, then go back again to your bed and
repeat the experiment.

5. When floating, does the physical body remain in the bed?

Samael Aun Weor: I want you to understand me; listen: it is
clear that if you float in the surrounding environment it
is because you are outside of your physical body. In this
concrete case you must understand that your body has
been left in bed and that you as soul are outside the body
and far from the bed.

6. When one floats one must think that one travels to a certain
place?

Samael Aun Weor: I want you to understand that this is not a
matter of thinking, but of doing, which is different. For
example, I see you seated on that chair; thus, if you *think*
that you are going to get up from that chair and go to
the street, however, you do not act, it is clear that you will
remain seated there on that chair; so, action is what is
needed: do you understand me?

7. This is what I like about Gnosis: here, everything that I do not understand is clearly explained to me.

Samael Aun Weor: Of course; we like exactness, precision in everything.

8. Can you narrate for us a concrete case of astral projection by will?

Samael Aun Weor: With great pleasure, distinguished young lady, I will narrate for you a personal case. I want to narrate for you my first astral projection. I was still very young when I resolved to astral project myself by will. I clearly remember that I put much attention to my slumber process, thus, when I felt myself dozing in that state of transition that exists between vigil and dream, I acted intelligently.

I did not situate myself to *think* that I was going to be astral projected, because it is obvious that if I had been thinking about it I would not have performed the longed-for experiment. I repeat: I acted; I got up with great smoothness from my own bed, and when doing so a very natural separation between the soul and the body took place; the soul remained outside and the body remained sleeping in the bed.

I went out of my house in a spontaneous and clear manner and then walked down a solitary street. I stopped on the next corner of the street; for few moments I reflected about where I should go; then I resolved to go to Europe.

It is obvious that I had to soar over the waters of the Atlantic Ocean; thus, floating wonderfully in the luminous space, I was filled with a happiness that is inconceivable for human beings, and finally I arrived at the city of Paris.

Thus, walking—or better said, floating in that luminous atmosphere—I instinctively felt the necessity of entering into a house.

I do not regret having entered into that house because within that mansion I encountered an initiate I had known in old reincarnations.

He was also outside his body; certainly I ascertained that his body was sleeping in the bed, and next to him I saw a woman and two children who also slept with him; I understood that these were his wife and children.

I affectionately greeted my friend and the soul of his wife, who was also outside her body; it is not irrelevant to also state that as the children were also sleeping, their souls were outside their bodies.

Those infantile souls began to be scared by my unusual presence; I then understood the necessity to withdraw in order to avoid the return of such frightened souls to their respective bodies; it is unquestionable that if this had happened, the children would have cried in bed and the weeping would have woken my friend and his wife; then the dialogue would have been suspended, since the soul of my friend as well as his wife would had been forced to penetrate in their respective bodies of bone and flesh.

Indeed, I understood all of this in thousandths of a second; thus, in order to avoid this problem, I proposed that my friend leave the house and go with me around the streets of Paris; my joy was great when he accepted.

Thus, together we went through the streets of that great city; I even advised him to return to the path, to enter the path of the Light; I also proposed that we visit a wonderful temple that exists in Germany, but regrettably, my friend declined the invitation stating that he could not because he had concentrated his attention on the problems of practical life, since he had a spouse and children, etc. I then said farewell to that Initiate and—soaring in the atmosphere—I passed over great walls and then soared over a highway, by a serpentine way full of curves, until I arrived at a wonderful temple.

In front of that sanctuary I saw many souls of different nationalities, people who during the hours of their sleep escaped from their dense body in order to arrive there.

So, all those people united in different groups were conversing amongst themselves; they spoke of the cosmos, of the laws, of reincarnations and Karma, the mysteries of life and death, etc.

I looked for a friend who was skillful in astral projection but I did not find him.

I then approached the threshold of the temple and saw an exquisite garden with delicious flowers that exhaled an inebriating perfume; at its depth, the silhouette of a splendid temple illuminated by the splendors of the stars stood out; I wanted to enter, but the guardian intervened and told me, "This is the temple of wisdom; withdraw, it is not time yet."

Thus, obeying his orders, I withdrew to a certain distance without moving too much away from the threshold. Then I examined myself; I observed my spiritual hands and feet and even had the luxury of comparing them with the hands and feet of my body of bones and flesh that I had left there in Latin America, the sacred land of the Aztecs, sleeping in the bed.

It is evident that the outcome of such comparisons originated the instantaneous return into my material physical vehicle that slept deeply, snoring in the bed; then I, astounded, woke up saying, "I was in the temple of the wisdom; what happiness, what joy."

Even today, I cannot forget the immaculate white light that was shining in that sanctuary; indeed, such a light did not seem to come from any physical lamp, since it projected itself from all parts and it did not make any type of shade.

9. Is it possible for one to travel to a place without already knowing that place?

> Samael Aun Weor: I went to such a divine temple and nevertheless, I did not know that place; I could say that a "superior telepathic sense"—or it is better to state to you, that my own Spirit guided me there.

10. When one does the astral projection voluntarily can one remember where one went upon waking?

> Samael Aun Weor: It is clear that if you do not remember, it is because you did not astral project by will; it seems impossible to me that a person who astral projects voluntarily— who leaves the body consciously, intentionally—will be unable to remember what he/she saw outside their body. For example, when you leave your house to go to the office and soon return from the office to your house, do you remember what you saw in the office, the work that you did, and the commands of your boss?

11. Yes, when I return to my house I remember everything that I did in the office.

> Samael Aun Weor: So then this case is similar, young lady. Remember that your physical body is a house of bones and flesh; thus, if you voluntarily leave that house you will then see many things, and if you voluntarily return, it is also obvious that you will remember everything that you saw and heard.

Ninth Chapter
Mystic Phenomena

1. On a certain occasion in the countryside when I was performing an exercise of meditation, I felt as if I was vibrating
while leaving the body; then, suddenly I felt that I was flying
at a great speed and arriving at Egypt in a couple of seconds.
I landed close to the Sphinx and felt the heat of the sand
in the soles of my feet, I was able to touch the enormous
decayed stones of that gigantic monument. It was a great
surprise for me to see such an open panorama and such a
vivid perception of the sky, as well as a tenuous breeze from
the Nile river that was blowing and moving some large, thin
palms.

After a brief rest, I felt myself driven by a special attraction that lifted me from the floor; thus, floating, I soared
approximately to the height of the nose of the Sphinx. In
the nose I found a small opening; I entered through it and
went down a set of steps that descended in very narrow
manner ending at a chamber guarded by a brown-skinned
guardian. He wore an apron and golden sandals. On his
head he had a hairstyle with a golden diadem that resem-
bled a cobra in the attitude of attack. In his right hand was
a lance that hindered my passage. His very penetrating eyes
were bluish green. He did not even pronounce a single word;
he only examined me and performed a greeting pass which
I answered; he smiled, took hold of the lance and with an
amiable reverence allowed me to pass; I then penetrated into
a great chamber where I heard very soft songs from a choir
chanting prayers in the form of delectable hymns.

There was a pink colored smoke from incense in the environment, which smelled like an extract of red roses and
which made my body vibrate from head to toes. There were
also many Egyptian symbols on the walls, which—in spite
of not understanding them—were very familiar to me. So,
after observing the rich decoration of that chamber, which

undoubtedly must be a very special temple, a gong sounded and three Masters appeared who had calm and venerable faces, yet very penetrating sight; two of them came dressed with yellow tunics and one with a very white tunic; after saluting me they welcomed me with a very fraternal hug.

Thereafter, they celebrated a Mass on an altar that was between two enormous columns and that had a great golden scarab that shone in the midst of the incense smoke. Then a crystalline water fountain, that I did not notice before, became illuminated; they guided me towards it, and in it I began to see my face as black and horribly bearded, like the face of an orangutan; then I saw many passages of my present life where I committed all types of sin; so, I ended up moaning and crying.

Later they admonished me and gave me advice in a symbolic manner. They gave me a scarab of solid gold; they put it on my right hand and closed it while pronouncing some words that I did not understand; then they told me to keep it and to become worthy of always having it by my side. Then, they blessed me and I returned to my body. Very impressed, I woke up instantaneously, without forgetting any detail to the present day. Could you tell me what happened to me and what all of this signifies for me?

Samael Aun Weor: I will gladly answer your question. Certainly, a rapturous projection of the soul clearly stands out with complete dazzling clarity. While you were meditating and praying, your body was left asleep and you as soul left the body and went to Egypt, the sacred land of the Pharaohs.

I want you to comprehend that you spiritually entered into the mysterious Temple of the Sphinx. It pleases me very much the fact that you discovered a secret door in the very nose of the Sphinx. It is obvious that it is not a physical, material door, it is rather a door invisible to the physical senses, but perfectly visible to the intelligence and the heart.

It is also obvious that the Temple of the Sphinx is not found in this physical world, since this is a temple invisible to the eyes of the flesh, but totally visible to the eyes of the Spirit.

What happened to you is something very similar to that experience of the Apostle Paul, who, as it is known, was taken to heaven and saw and heard ineffable things, which people do not comprehend.

There is no doubt that you were initiated in the Egyptian mysteries in a previous existence, and due to this you were called to that temple. For that reason, for the call that they performed when you were in meditation, you went precisely there.

You spiritually attended an Egyptian ritual; you saw and heard the priests of the temple; you listened to sublime hymns and saw in the water your sinning "I" and all of those crimes that you have committed. There is no doubt that you saw yourself very ugly; this is how, because of sins, one becomes very horrendous.

They delivered you a sacred scarab of pure gold: this is a wonderful symbol of the sanctified soul; that is all.

Sir, I hope that you comprehended me. Now, it is indispensable for you to resolve to follow the path of sanctity, to repent of all of your errors.

2. On another occasion—together with a spiritual friend of much wisdom, whom I love like a father—I was performing exercises of meditation in a forest of the vicinities of the town of Cuernavaca, Mexico, and I had the following experience.

We both sat in that yogic asana well-known as "the lotus flower" [padmasana] and did some breathing exercises; thereafter, we entered into silence and meditation. Then, immediately I felt transported to the Himalayan Mountains, to the area of Tibet. There was a tremendous cold in that place where the acute howl of winds was heard. I also saw some armed Chinese soldiers walking around those inhospitable places. I arrived at a somewhat cloudy plain where a majestic walled construction was little by little exposed,

which had an enormous wooden gate held by iron nails
forged centuries ago; however, its entrance was guarded by
two Tibetan soldiers, who when approaching indicated for
me to stop, and told me to wait for a while in order to verify
if I had the right to pass.

Moments later, they received a message, then the squeaking
noise of the hinges of the enormous gate was heard; thus,
they allowed me to pass. The city seemed to me, at first
glance, simultaneously heavenly and spectacular, since the
whiteness of its marble shone together with its delectable
gardens, with flowers of an indescribable beauty and shrubs
of green and yellow tonalities never shown on the earth. I
walked by broad stairs that had handrails with columns
turned in beautiful marble figures and which led me to a
small square that had a crystalline and vaporous water fountain; it was small and it had a beautifully sculptured boy
in the center who poured from a pitcher water that never
finished. Then, I turn towards the right and walked towards
the vestibule of an horizontally extended building that had
seven marble columns beautifully decorated; when I was
observing the corridor, I began to listen to angelical choirs
whose sound manifested a luminous figure who inspired
awe: this was no less than the figure of the Master Jesus, the
Christ, and I, when seeing him, felt faint; yet, he fixed his
gaze upon me, and a smile of love and fraternity was visible
on his face. Thereafter he immediately approached me and
put his right hand on my forehead while pronouncing the
following words: "Go and teach to all nations that I will be
with all of you."

Later, we walked by other corridors and we met other great
Masters, amongst which I recognized the Master Samael
Aun Weor, to whom the Christ called in a loud voice in
order to recommend that he watch and instruct my humble
person. Thereafter, the Christ called other students and
Masters dressed in white who were close to us; then with
special prayers and mantras he blessed all of us. He personally dismissed the Master Samael and me, while seeing how

that very magnificent place was disappearing from our sight.

When I returned to my body, I opened my eyes and saw that my friend was not awake yet, but a minute later he awoke and we commented upon the lived experiences.

How is it that a humble Gnostic student without any type of merits had so wonderful an experience, and had entrusted to him this so delicate mission?

Samael Aun Weor: With great pleasure I will answer your question. Now you can see what meditation and prayer is. If a person of good will delivers himself to prayer and meditation, he can have the joy of reaching ecstasy. Then the soul leaves the body—as we have already explained many times—and travels to any remote place of the Earth or the infinite.

In this concrete case of yours, it is clear that you went to Tibet, and penetrated into a secret temple where you could see the Masters of humanity and our Lord the Christ. Do not forget that the soul in prayer, in ecstasy, can see the Christ; you experienced this bliss and there is no doubt that the Lord entrusted you to teach the Gnostic doctrine to all your fellowmen.

It is obvious that I must give you the Gnostic teachings; this is why you saw and heard that the Lord commanded me to instruct you.

Tenth Chapter
Mystic Experiences of a Neophyte

1. One night of 1966 while utilizing one of the practices of astral projection, I managed to leave my body consciously; then I felt a very special freedom, an indescribable joy. Thus, like a bird I flew to another planet, which was unknown to me, but very much like the planet Earth, since I saw enormous green forests filled with pines and a log cabin within which I saw some people waving their hands aloft to get my attention; I descended and with great surprise found that the Master Samael Aun Weor was there with some relatives and some of his disciples, who greeted me with a very warm hug and a very special joy that I cannot describe.

Thereafter, the Master invited me to walk in the forest until we arrived at a stone bridge, where he explained that this planet was the Moon of the former round, when it had inhabitants, animals, and vegetation. So, that was the ancient Earth-Moon or Mother Earth-Moon; he showed rivers, mountains, and great seas to me.

Could you explain to me how it is possible to visit another planet back in time, like in that remote epoch?

Samael Aun Weor: Now you see, respectable gentleman, what a conscious projection is; through it, the soul can transport itself to other planets and know many mysteries. Listen: you were actually projected as Soul-Spirit to that satellite—or whatever you want to call it—that shines in the starry nights.

Certainly, you found my Spirit there at that mentioned bridge; however, it is obvious that what you saw—namely, the bridge, the river, the vegetation, etc.—corresponds to an extremely ancient past, because presently the moon is a corpse.

It is good for you to know that the worlds, the people, the plants, and the animals, are born, grow, age, and die. So, in name of truth I must tell you that the moon is now a corpse. Nonetheless, such a satellite had life in abundance throughout its childhood, its youth, its maturity, but it aged and finally died.

The soul can see not only the future and the present, but also the past. Thus, what you saw exactly corresponds to that ancient time in which the Moon had mighty rivers, deep seas, exuberant vegetation, volcanoes in eruption, vegetal, animal, and human life.

I want you know that the Selenites existed, since the Moon had seven human root races through successive historical periods. The first root race were giants and the last ones were Lilliputians—in other words, pygmies. So, we could classify the last human families who lived on the Moon as human ants; do not be surprised by what I am stating to you, since this is what happens on every planet: the first root races are giant and the last extremely small.

Congratulations for having remembered what you saw and heard on the Moon.

2. In the month of July 1969, Master Samael Aun Weor, his family, a friend, another disciple, and this humble servant had the opportunity to visit a town of the state of Hidalgo. We departed in a car during a very rainy and slightly cold afternoon with the purpose of studying an archaeological zone; however, we thought that it was not going to be possible to visit such a place, since a strong rain was pouring along the highway and there was very little visibility.

We traversed almost all of the way, and when arriving saw with surprise how the sky of the town we were heading towards was becoming very clear while black clouds were gathered around it. Thus, we could practically visit the archaeological zone in its entirety.

Then, I noticed that the Master Samael made some instantaneous concentrations, and afterwards commented to his wife that permission had been given; then he asked me if I noticed the phenomenon that took place. My answer was affirmative, since it was obvious that he had requested the end of the rain.

After our visit, he indicated for us to go into the car and instantaneously the rain began to pour. Could you tell me how this miracle was possible?

Samael Aun Weor: Is it good for you to know that the four elements—fire, air, water, and earth—are densely populated by the elemental creatures of nature. What I am telling you may appear very odd to you; however, at all times in our history there have existed traditions about fairies, nymphs, nereids, sylphs, elves, etc.,

Well then, those are the elementals; they are called elementals because they live in the elements.

The pygmies, for example, live within rocks of the earth; the salamanders live in the fire; the sylphs in the air, the clouds; and the nereids in the water.

Skeptical people do not accept anything of this, but I believe that you are a person who has faith and this is why I will explain and answer your question with great pleasure.

By means of certain secret formulas, my own Spirit gave orders to the sylphs who live in the clouds for them to move those clouds away. Nevertheless, you must not ignore that the waters are controlled by the undines. By propelling special psychic currents, the sylphs can take or move the clouds away from some place and thereby also move away the undines of the waters; thus the rain momentarily can be moved away; however, we the Initiates only perform this in very special cases, since otherwise disorder in nature would result.

When a Gnostic Initiate performs a miracle like that, he always does it with the permission of Superior Beings.

The miracle that you witnessed was necessary, because it was necessary for us to study some monoliths from Tula, which, by the way, were quite remarkable.

Pyramid of the Sun

3. In a practice in which I wanted to remember my past lives, such as you have taught us, I had the following experiences:

I saw myself in the pyramids of Teotihuacán at the time of the Aztecs; thus, where the citadel is located there was a great multitude that shouted great acclamations and vociferations, since along the "Avenue of the Dead" were reunited people of the town, soldiers, and politicians richly adorned with plumes, bracelets, sandals, and ornaments of gold and jewelry.

Along the avenue, I along with several prisoners tied by their hands and necks, surrounded by several soldiers dressed as tiger and eagle knights, walked towards the foot of the Pyramid of the Sun, where a great bonfire was burning, and when arriving at the platform they placed us in a line. A priest made a signal and everybody became silent; then they began to sound the "chirimías" and "teponaztlis"; later, came maidens dancing with indescribable flamboyance.

When the dances concluded, twelve elders came who performed a type of court-martial; then they judged us. Thereafter, they blindfolded us, and forced us to ascend the steps of the pyramid. Along the way, some slipped and fell; since we listened to the noise and the shouts of pain, I remember that I felt the steps to be very narrow, since scarcely half of my foot fit there. Then there were some prayers, invocations, and offerings when arriving at the superior platform, where finally we were sacrificed to the God Huichilopotxtli.

Could explain to me what happened? Is that a reincarnation or a return?

Samael Aun Weor: With the longing of remembering your past lives while in meditation, you became a little drowsy and then your soul escaped from your body of bones and flesh; thereafter, the different scenes and memories of the past came to you. I invite you to comprehend that indeed you were an Aztec citizen, an inhabitant of ancient Mexico.

Obviously, you saw how the Aztecs judged their many delinquents and how later they sacrificed them to the Gods. Therefore, not all of those who were immolated at the altar of human sacrifices were innocent people; human sacrifices existed in the pre-Columbian Mexico.

Eleventh Chapter

Negotiations

1. I have a business, and lately the economic situation has become very difficult for me; my store goes terribly; many of my clients have gone. What I must do?

Samael Aun Weor: First of all, my dear friend, I must tell you that you need to keep forty days of absolute sexual abstention, because I understand that you have had a very profane life; you have been an awful fornicator—that is, you have clumsily spent your sexual energies.

It is indispensable—it is urgent—for you to comprehend the intimate relationship between the sexual organs and the pineal gland.

Do not be surprised by what I am stating to you; such a small gland is located in the superior part of the brain.

Any Gnostic student knows very well that in our organism we have a complete wireless system. The solar plexus —located at the region of the navel—is the telepathic receiver-antenna that catches the mental waves of our friends and enemies, and transmits them to the mind. The pineal gland is the transmitter of thought, which transmits waves to different people and places.

It is clear that the great vendors, the great dealers of all times, have such a gland very developed.

When the sexual energy is squandered, then the pineal gland weakens, degenerates; then, one no longer can emit mental waves with force. Thus, failure in business is the outcome.

Since you are a profane person who knows nothing about our esoteric studies, the only thing that I can advise you is to keep at least forty days of absolute sexual abstention in order to accumulate sexual energies and give force to your pineal gland; thus, this is how your economic situation will improve; it will be a favorable change.

And Moses' anger waxed hot, and he cast the tables out of his hands, and brake them beneath the mount.

Exod. XXXII. 19.

In addition, I advise you to carry sulfur within your shoes. Do not be surprised! The ethereal emanations of sulfur will clean your personal atmosphere.

You must know that through fornication many invisible larvae are formed around your aura. There exist various species of larvae, but with the emanations of sulfur those filthy larvae are disintegrated and your atmosphere is clarified.

Moreover, it is convenient for you to cleanse the atmosphere of the place where you have your business; so, perform sulfur smudges (a smoky, sulfur fire to drive the larvae away from there); do this for about nine days. Afterwards, perform smudges with sugar for another nine days, this in order to sweeten the atmosphere, to make it pleasant.

We are talking here about occultism, and I think that you comprehend me, because you need to improve your business.

2. Could you indicate to me what I can do in order to prosper? I sell articles in many towns of the states of Mexico, so, I do not have a fix placed of business, and there are months where I cannot profit anything.

Samael Aun Weor: I comprehend your situation, my friend. With all sincerity I can tell you that when one fulfills exactly the Ten Commandments of the law of God, when one prays daily to the Father who is in secret, it is clear that any situation improves. Then, our Heavenly Father grants us everything; we lack nothing. But when one goes bad, when one does not really fulfill the Ten Commandments, when one does not deliver himself to the Father, then the Father is absent and one falls into disgrace.

Follow my advice: make many works of charity, make a vow of chastity, bathe your body with aromatic herbs, such as peppermint, chamomile, eucalyptus, walnut, etc. Use these plants for forty days in your daily bath and, I repeat, make works of charity by tons; only thus will your economic situation improve.

3. Well then, but what do you understand by chastity?

Samael Aun Weor: My friend, here, I am not going to explain the **Arcanum A.Z.F** of our Gnostic studies to you, because you would not understand it; this is only an elementary book for those people who never have studied our other books. I will limit myself to tell you that you must keep forty days of sexual abstention in thought, word, and actions; that is all. However, if you wish to penetrate a little further into our studies, then read our advanced books, such as the *The Perfect Matrimony,* and many others.

4. Could you explain to me the works of charity that I can do?

Samael Aun Weor: It is good for you to know that works of charity are works of mercy, namely: give food to the hungry, give drink to the thirsty, dress the naked, teach those who do not know, heal the ill, etc.

5. Could you tell me when can I make a work of charity and when not, and to whom?

Samael Aun Weor: One is not a judge in order to judge any one else; besides, charity does not need a judge. Charity is a matter of common sense. To give food to the hungry is something very humane, because even the prisoners have to eat, otherwise they would die of hunger. To give drink to the thirsty is something very logical, since it would be cruel to deny a glass of water to a thirsty person. To give a shirt to the naked is something very natural; to console the afflicted one is very humane; so, we do not needed judges for that. Nevertheless, it would be an absurdity to give alcohol to the drunkard, or to lend a weapon to an assassin.

Love is law, but love with cognizance!

Twelfth Chapter

The Law of Freewill

1. I want to ask you a favor: it so happens that my husband has been taken from me by another woman; I undergo the unspeakable, and do not know what to do.

Since you know the occult sciences, it seems to me that you could fix my problem. I know that you have a wonderful mental force and therefore, you can dominate the mind of the neighbor, to entice the beloved one, to place him at my feet by means of magic.

What would be the price of your work? I can pay you whatever the price may be.

Samael Aun Weor: I believe you are mistaken, lady; I am not a black magician. To use the forces of the mind in order to subjugate others, in order to enslave them, in order to force them, is violence, and any violent act is black magic.

Each to his own. Nobody has the right to intrude into the private affairs of other people; it is absurd to want to dominate others.

When will people learn to respect the free will of others? Do you believe perhaps that one can force somebody—to force him with impunity—to love other people, just by our whim? It is necessary for you to know that these types of actions of black magic are chastised with very severe punishments. The Angels of Destiny are not willing to forgive these types of crimes; therefore, if you continue on that path you will receive your punishment.

There exist in this world many people who dedicate themselves to witchcraft, to sorcery, to black magic. Thousands of sorcerers live on that filthy business, thus, it is clear that such people do not progress because black magic brings misery, hunger, nakedness, supreme pain.

2. Does the punishment of the people who dedicate themselves to witchcraft also reach their children?

> Samael Aun Weor: Is clear that the environment of black magicians is usually disastrous; the children of these tenebrous ones are also tenebrous. It is evident that the lost souls search for black magicians in order to have them as their progenitors or terrestrial parents; then it is not odd that the children of the perverse ones can be perverse also, and fall into misfortune.
>
> It is regrettable for people to not understand the necessity of respecting the free will of others. There always exists the ominous tendency of dominating others, to want to impose our ideas onto our neighbors by force, to try to force others to do whatever our own whim wants them to do; all of this is severely punished with tears, misery, and supreme pain.

3. Why is it that those black magicians consider that they are performing good deeds to humanity since, although they collect payments, they are helping them to solve their problems?

> Samael Aun Weor: I what you to know that the logic of absurdity exists. For the tenebrous ones, white is black and vice versa; remember that the pathway that leads to the abyss is paved with good intentions.
>
> Letters from many places that are soliciting these type of service are constantly mailed to me; indeed, it is painful, but this humanity has to be pitied. One is giving a divine message to the people, yet instead of worrying about the study of such a message, the only thing that occurs to women is to write to me so that I will secure their husbands to them, or if they are men, so that I will dominate the mind of the woman they covet, or that I will intrude in other people's thoughts in order for this fellow to pay money to this other fellow, etc., etc.
>
> Indeed, all this causes deep pain to me, since they do not write me in order to request esoteric guidance, or to clarify the teachings, but to request domination of others;

thus, this is the state in which this humanity is. For this reason I prefer that they do not write to me, because I am only concerned with the teachings, concerned with how to show the path of liberation, concerned about how to indicate the door that leads to the true happiness of the Spirit; regrettably, the multitudes do not want to understand this.

People exist whom have highly priced the power of mental suggestion; they collect so many dollars by each suggestion, so many other dollars in order to place a "spirit" (as the spiritualists state) to the adored or beloved one so he or she can love them, so that the ones they covet can leave the other person with whom they sleep within their arms, thus, they can come crying to their house, and etc., and other etceteras.

It is clear that all those filthy businesses are abysmal, tenebrous, and those who exert them with good or bad devotion will inevitably enter the abyss where only weeping and gnashing of teeth are heard.

4. I foretell with cards and I can swear that I say the truth to people; I help them with their problems, although I collect from them because that is my way of living. Do you think that I am behaving uprightly?

Samael Aun Weor: You have a horrible way of living; you are in fact a pythoness, a hag. Do you think perhaps that you can utter the truth with the devil within, exactly within the very kingdom of your heart?

You know very well—and it is convenient for you not to ignore once and for all—that you carry the sinning "I" of mortals—that is, Satan himself—within your own heart.

Can a person who has not yet arrived at sanctity be illuminated? The very fact of receiving payment for preaching or foretelling is already is a crime. You might think that what you do is good, but do not be surprised; in the abyss live many anchorites, penitents, wizards, sorcerers, fortune tellers, who feel themselves to be martyrs and who also think they are behaving in an upright way.

5. Then can you tell me if my children and all those to whom I have taught my beliefs are going bad?

Samael Aun Weor: Since it is concerned with beliefs related with divination, foretelling, etc., I must tell you that they are going bad. I repeat: it is not possible to know the destiny of others if we do not know our own destiny, and it is not possible to know our own destiny if we have not yet arrived at the awakening of our consciousness. Such an awakening is impossible if we previously do not annihilate the sinning "I" (our defects).

6. In spite of having studied in esoteric schools for many years and having abstained from sex although being married, do you think that there is no salvation for me?

Samael Aun Weor: I think that you are going very badly, since you are married and you have rejected the "Consolator" about which Jesus the Christ spoke to us: I am referring to the Holy Spirit. It is clear that the Holy Spirit is in the sex; thus, knowing how to handle it, one can arrive at illumination, but you reject it and do not even fulfill your sexual duties with your husband. So, do you still believe that you are behaving uprightly?

You might have received a pseudo-occultist or pseudo-esoteric type of information, yet you have realized nothing; the sinning "I" is very alive in you: recognize it and repent; study our books and practice.

7. Well, I exert all types of works; I fix spouses to other people; I make people to come to others by force, etc., etc., etc., and I am doing very well economically since I make a lot of money, then what? What could you tell me about this?

Samael Aun Weor: Misery, in this case, will come to you, just a little bit later. Meanwhile, keep bearing the moral sufferings that you are undergoing—that, by the way, are not very pleasant: remember that you have an ill son with epilepsy. These types of patients are indeed possessed by demons. Do not you understand that? Or do you not want to understand it? Understand: the fate that is reserved for you will be the abyss and the Second Death.

Thirteenth Chapter

Practical Magic

1. Because of my sister's birthday, I went to her house, where I had not been for long while because I only visit her every eight days. I found her to be very sick and could not tell what her illness was. She explained to me that for a long time she felt like that only at night, and that she could not sleep because of shortness of breath. When she wanted to read a certain esoteric book that I gave her, she became so ill that she could not read it, except by reciting the Conjuration of the Seven that I had given her and by invoking you.

Thus, when seeing her so ill, I felt within my heart the urge to cleanse her with two eggs while reciting the Conjuration of the Seven of Solomon the Wise that you had taught to us. A few minutes later she felt better and could breathe perfectly again. I wish you to tell me if I proceeded well and the cause of that disease.

Samael Aun Weor: There is no doubt that the tenebrous ones usually attack the people who look for the Path of Light. It is clear that the powers of darkness live in the invisible world; they watch, thus, when they see that a soul tries to escape from their claws, then they make efforts in order to turn them aside, in order to move them away from the Luminous Path.

You proceeded uprightly by healing your sister. There is no doubt that when the egg is used in the way you did, it certainly has wonderful, magical powers; it permits the elimination of certain larvae and malignant fluids that accumulate in the atmosphere of people, thus causing them diverse maladies.

It is necessary for the people who read these lines to know the Conjuration of the Seven of Solomon the Wise, which was the conjuration you recited in order to drive away the tenebrous ones who were attacking your sister.

The conjuration is as follows:

CONJURATION OF THE SEVEN

In the name of Michael, may Jehovah command thee and drive thee hence, Chavajoth!

In the name of Gabriel, may Adonai command thee and drive thee hence, Bael!

In the name of Raphael, begone before Elial, Samgabiel!

By Samael Sabaoth, and in the name of Elohim Gibor, get thee hence, Andrameleck!

By Zachariel et Sachiel-Meleck, be obedient unto Elvah, Sanagabril!

By the divine and human name of Shaddai, and by the sign of the Pentagram which I hold in my right hand, in the name of the angel Anael, by the power of Adam and Eve, who are Yod-HaVah, begone Lilith! Let us rest in peace, Nahemah!

By the holy Elohim and by the names of the Genii Cashiel, Sehaltiel, Aphiel, and Zarahiel, at the command of Orifiel, depart from us Moloch. We deny thee our children to devour!

Amen. Amen. Amen.

It is necessary to memorize this conjuration and use it in the moments when it is necessary; you knew how to use it precisely at the right moment.

2. The next day I returned to her house with another Gnostic brother, because I saw she was very gloomy. Thus, together we burned sulfur, frankincense, and myrrh throughout the house; we placed there an Esoteric Pentagram that you had magnetized for me and we performed chains in order to summon all the Masters of the White Brotherhood so that they would help us. Did we proceed well?

Samael Aun Weor: The smudges are very useful for the cleansing of the atmosphere of a house. Sulfur, for example, disintegrates larvae; other smudges are necessary, yet, one must know how to use them. You have to burn sulfur for nine days in a row, in order to purify the atmosphere of that house and to cleanse it from astral larvae; later, you should have continued with the other smudges, because frankincense and myrrh are very useful, but they must not be mixed with sulfur, since they are incompatible.

Count Cagliostro used to invoke the four saints or four angels who, located in the four cardinal points of the Earth, govern the destiny of human beings.

There is no doubt that Count Cagliostro also used these other cleansing smudges, namely, he offered laurel [bay leaf] to the Genie of the Light who lives in the East, myrtle to the Angel of the West, frankincense to the King of the North, myrrh to the King of the South. So, in a case of serious necessity one can invoke these four saints by offering to each of them their correspondent smudge offering and requesting with all of our heart the yearned for assistance.

ESOTERIC PENTAGRAM

ELIPHAS LEVI (ALPHONSE LOUIS CONSTANT)

Fourteenth Chapter
Occult Medicine

1. Master, what can you tell me about healing from a distance?

Samael Aun Weor: Well, I constantly receive mail from different places of the world soliciting such treatments. In our replies we limit ourselves to Spiritual Medicine; we indicate the precise hour in which they can concentrate on us, that is to say, to think on us, to invoke us.

It is clear that we attend to the patients spiritually, and some times we even become visible before them.

As a general rule, we instruct them as follows: we tell them to ignite three fires at a certain convinient hour; we advise them to place a glass of water before those three fires or candles; we indicate that, after half an hour of concentration on us, they must drink the water.

It is evident that within the water we deposit certain substances that when absorbed usually perform wonderful healings within the interior of the organism.

In these healing treatments, several Masters cooperate, such as Paracelsus, Hilarion, Saint Raphael and some others. We do not always indicate to them specific concentration in Samael, since "I have much work to do"; thus, we also indicate to them for the same purpose any one of the other Masters.

What is important is for the patient to have faith, because faith performs miracles; as Christ already stated: "Have faith as a grain of mustard seed, ye shall say unto this mountain, Remove hence to yonder place; and it shall remove; and nothing shall be impossible unto you." Faith has a wonderful solar power with which many prodigies can be performed.

Our healing system is spiritual. It does not conflict with physicians; everyone can have faith in our methods and consult their doctor in the physical world.

2. Can the ill be cured by means of these methods?

Samael Aun Weor: It is clear that the Masters of medicine heal the vital body by applying medicines to it; thus, later on the outcome is the healing of the physical organism. Nevertheless, there exist very severe karmic diseases, which are the outcome of evil actions committed by the soul in former lives; thus, when the punishment of these souls is very severe, the treatment of their bodies becomes impossible. Nonetheless, the Masters of medicine always attend and try to save the patient.

3. Is it possible to be healed without the need of conventional medical attention?

Samael Aun Weor: When the person does not owe a very severe karma, the Masters of medicine can cure the patient, even when the latter does not consult any conventional doctor.

4. Are all diseases karmic?

Samael Aun Weor: Distinguished young lady, there is no need to exaggerate this matter: not all the diseases are karmic; this is why many patients heal quickly with our psychic or spiritual procedures. However, it is convenient to know that in these times many unknown diseases are appearing, which are the frightful outcome of human perversity, and such diseases are usually lethal.

5. Can you tell me if the so called "evil eye" disease exists?

Samael Aun Weor: I must tell you that thousands of children die in the cities because of the evil eye. It so happens that in "super-civilized countries" people do not believe in such a disease and therefore mortality increases in an alarming manner.

Any person with an unconscious hypnotic force can—in an involuntarily manner—hurt the vital body of a child when staring at him/her, thus, the outcome does delay much in appearing: soon the creature appears with great dark circles under their eyes, vomiting, fever, diarrhea, etc. Modern physicians usually diagnose "intestinal infection" and prescribe many antibiotics, fluids, etc., but children instead of healing, they get worse and die.

6. What can be done in these cases in order to heal them?

Samael Aun Weor: The best thing is to perform strong magnetic passes from bottom to top over the face and eyelids of the child, with the firm purpose of eliminating the tenebrous vital fluids. It is convenient to ignite a taper, candle, or oil lamp, and to read to the ill children the Conjuration of the Seven of Solomon the Wise, as it is already written in this elementary book for introducing Gnosis [see the previous chapter]. One must also bless with the sign of the cross the forehead, the chest, the head, and the back of the young patient while reading to him the four gospels.

7. To read the four gospels is very long; could this be somehow abbreviated?

Samael Aun Weor: Yes, you can read the blessings of the Lord [Matthew 5] with true faith, so that the healing force is sufficiently strong in order to evacuate the bad fluids accumulated in the organism of the patient, so that this can be healed.

8. Are there diseases caused by witchcraft?

Samael Aun Weor: The world is full of them, distinguished young lady; I could mention innumerable cases, but they would not fit within the covers of this book. First of all, I must tell you that the exact diagnosis is necessary; only thus is it possible to cure.

Unfortunately, the healers who really know how to diagnose a disease caused by witchcraft are very rare. I am going to mention a very special case narrated by Waldemar the wise; I will write this between quotations, because I do not like to adorn myself with other people's feathers, yet since this narration is really sensational, it is good for our readers to know it.

"One of the most intriguing cases of vampirical jealousy was experienced by the French occultist investigator Eliphas Levi (Alphonse Louis Constant).

"During his stay in London, Levi started a friendship with a young Duke, in whose house he was invited almost every day. The Duke had been married a short time ago to a young and extraordinarily beautiful French princess, and that against the desire of his Protestant family, since the young lady was a devoted Catholic.

"The Duke, as Levi verified, had for many years lived a somewhat frivolous life—that is to say, as a libertine—and for a long time had taken as a lover a young Italian girl, a dancer of ballet, who finally he left, since, in fact, he truly loved his wife.

"On a certain afternoon the Duchess become sick; thus, she had to stay in bed. The doctors diagnosed the beginning of a pregnancy, but soon determined that the weakness she suffered must have its origin in another cause. Although the Duke called the most famous doctors of London for consultation, they were before an enigma, since they used diverse remedies but without any success.

"An old French abbot also frequented the Duke's palace. The abbot already knew the princess of Paris, and he found special affability in talking with Eliphas Levi on metaphysical problems, in which he was also interested for decades, and not only theoretically.

"On a certain night they both remained alone in the hall, since the worried Duke had to stay next to his ill wife. It was a cold and humid night; outside, the famous London fog dimmed the light of the street lamps. Suddenly, the Abbot held the hand of Levi and said to him with a low voice, 'Listen, dear friend, I would like to speak about something to you. Can I be assured of your complete discretion?' Levi responded affirmatively, and the Abbot continued, 'I have every reason to suspect that the disease of the Duchess is not natural. I have known Mildred since her childhood and she was always the most healthy girl you can imagine. But now she languishes and gets weaker day by day; it seems as if she was bleeding mysteriously...'

"Do you believe that she is under the influence of some dark power, that there is sorcery in this matter?" Levi asked.

"'I trust my inner voice very much, and for that reason I would dare to state that this disease has something that is not as it should be. Do you want to help me to break the spell?'

"'With pleasure.'

"'Well, in that case we must not waste time. I would be thankful if you would come to my home at half an hour before midnight in order to perform a conjuration together. I will try to intercept the tenebrous power. Perhaps we will get an answer from beyond...'

"After this conversation, Eliphas Levi hired a carriage and went to his home, where he had to wash, shave, and change his clothes from head to toes, because the spirits of the middle zone, who were those whom the abbot thought to invoke, demand from their invokers the most scrupulous cleanliness. Clothing also had to be in accordance with their nature; they did not tolerate any fabric made from animals, therefore wool as well as animal skin shoes were discarded.

"Since the house of the abbot was to the northeast, in Hampstead Heath, and Eliphas lived in Russell Court, the distance between them was considerable; thus, Eliphas had to make his thorough cleanliness with certain haste if he wanted to be with the abbot at the suitable hour.

"Thus, about forty minutes before midnight Levi arrived at Hampstead Heath. The abbot in person, dressed in white, opened the door and led him by a high staircase to a chamber that was at the end of the corridor of the first floor. There, the eyes of Eliphas first had to become accustomed to the dark: little bluish and trembling flames were releasing incense that smelled of amber and musk.

"Within that vague light, Eliphas observed a great circular table in the center of the room, and on top of that table was an inverted crucifix, a symbol of the phallus. Next to that table was a thin little man. 'He is my servant,' whispered the abbot, 'since as you already know the quantity of three people are indispensable for these invocations. You must begin with the first invocation.' This request on the part of the abbot was more than a courtesy; the powers of the middle zone could become angry and seek revenge on the owner of the house until causing his death, for having allowed the reduction of the harmony of their sphere by an incompetent intruder. So, when granting the invocation to his friend, he was indicating that he considered Eliphas to be a Master of first rank in magic. And such a supposition was indeed justified: if anyone could successfully execute— with a clear head, without fear, with a pure heart, and a will fortified by numerous tests—the millenarian ceremonies of sacred magic, it was this man, who in the kingdom of the spirits exerted as much dominion as in the kingdom of its incarnated creatures and adepts.

"Within the veil of the smoke, Eliphas very instinctively extended the hand to the left, where there had to be the container with the blessed water collected on one full moon night from a cistern, guarded, while praying over it for twenty-one nights.

"Next, he sprinkled water towards the four corners of the room; the abbot who served as an acolyte waved the censer. Blurry figures began to form within the smoke, and at the same time, a icy cold seemed to appear from the ground and which reached even to the end of their hair, making breathing difficult for them.

"Next, Eliphas Levi pronounced with great force the words of the invocation. Suddenly, the walls of the room seemed to withdraw and an abyss was opened before them as if threatening to devour them, infinity, and astral: resplendencies of a sparkling luminosity shone; they covered their eyes in order not to offend the invoked spirit with an indiscreet glance. Then with a strong voice Levi asked for the cause of the Duchess Mildred's disease; but he did not receive an answer. The vapors of the smoke thickened in such a way that they threatened to deprive their senses. Then, hurrying to the window, Eliphas suddenly heard a voice, which, although was strong and resonant, seemed to come from the deepest inner part of himself and which filled all the space of his soul. What the voice shouted to him was so frightful that his legs refused to move, so he remained petrified on the same spot.

"Precipitately, the Abbot went to his side next to the window, but his trembling hands, without force, did not manage to open the pin. The servant, who had passively attended the invocation, was lying unconscious on the ground.

"Finally, Eliphas left his numbness and broke the window with the crucifix, absorbing with joy—together with the abbot—the fresh air of the night, especially he—who bathed, so to speak, his febrile head in the humid fog—since, through all his nerves darted the frightful accusation that the mysterious spirit had sent with unequivocal clarity against him.

"When he finally recovered a little, he returned to the room. The smoke had dissolved in the interval, and the pale candle continued burning tenuously. The very pale abbot with wide eyes contemplated Eliphas and stammered, 'Are you really guilty, my friend? I cannot believe it.'

"'So you have heard the answer of the spirit.'

"The abbot, as if overwhelmed, in a gesture of assent dropped the head, '...Yes...,' he slightly whispered.

"'I swear to you,' said Levi with vehemence, 'that I have taken the symbol with pure hands, that I have never committed a crime in my life! I swear to you that I am not stained with blood.' When uttering these words, he approached the lamp, so that the brilliance of the lamp completely fell upon him.

"Then the frightened abbot pointed with his finger to Eliphas' jaw and the chest of his shirt. 'There... look at yourself in the mirror...' said the abbot, taking the hand his friend and leading him before a great mirror that hung on a wall in the next room. Thus, there Eliphas saw a scratch upon his chin, with some little drops of dry blood; other little drops of dry blood also appeared on his shirt. He must have cut himself when shaving so hastily... Thus, the answer of the spirit was perfectly explained: 'I do not talk with any one who is stained with blood.'

"Levi felt as if his heart was relieved from many weights. The abbot, however, seemed more overwhelmed and dropped himself on a sofa, convulsively contracting his shoulders and hiding his face between his hands. Levi tried to calm the old man, but he rejected him, saying, 'I am concerned for the wretched Mildred; each hour her life is consumed. Otherwise, we could again invoke the spirit after three times twenty-one days, with the due offerings and plagiaries... but it is too much time, because in the interval Mildred will die.'

"Levi did not know how to respond, thus, a dense silence loomed, which the abbot cut when he rose and walked with vacillating steps from one side to the other of the room. 'It does not matter what the cost might be, I must obtain an answer at whatever cost...! Promise me, my friend, that you will not abandon me.'

"A vaporous determination was visible in the glance of the old man; so, in order to tranquilize him, Eliphas responded to him: 'I gave you my word to place myself as a magician. Thus, since the objective has not yet been obtained, I sustain my given word.'

"'Then stay here, and within twelve hours we will perform another conjuration; I will invoke the spirits of the low zone...'

"Eliphas then was frightened; had this old man become crazy? 'What.... what did you say...? A son of the Church wants to make contact with the infernal spirits? No, that is not even in the intention of the devoted Duchess! Resign to it, do not risk your soul.'

It is obvious that to invoke demons is black magic. It is obvious that black magic brings physical and moral hunger, nakedness, diseases, and calamities.

"There was such a very icy firmness in the words and gestures of the abbot that Eliphas felt that any objection would be in vain. Thus, against his will, although by loyalty to the given word, he accepted the requirement of his friend.

"So, Eliphas remained as a guest in the house and, because of the extraordinarily tense and tiring conjuration, he slept so heavily and deeply that he awoke late in the morning.

"The day passed with the due purifications and plagiaries. At night, Eliphas received the appropriate clothes and the requirements for the service of the Devil. The abbot had already stated to him that although he would attend him as an acolyte, he would not take an active part in the invocation; so he dressed also with the prescribed clothes.

What happened later is something that frankly in no way do I want to transcribe, because there is responsibility in the word; it is preferable to shut up in this case. "Silence is the eloquence of wisdom."

It is obvious that if one transcribes tenebrous paragraphs, one then becomes an accomplice to the crime; this is as much as to teach black magic to people.

Luckily, the invocators of the present story did not manage to make the invoked demons visible and tangible. The only thing that they attained was that a salamander—or small, innocent creature of the fire—appeared within the wall.

> "The abbot, pulling together all of his forces, asked for the ailment of the Duchess.

> "'Batrachians!' The salamander said with an infantile voice, and at the same moment it disappeared.

> "Eliphas then saw the abbot stagger and collapse to the ground.

> "Eliphas took his thin body in his arms and took him to the dormitory, where he undressed the old man and placed him in the bed, going soon to look for the servant who brought some relief. When returning, he found that the abbot had returned to himself completely, but his aspect was that of a downcast man who seemed to have aged many years.

It is obvious that the abbot was performing superhuman efforts in order to save the Duchess.

> "'All has been useless!' said the abbot with feeble voice, 'wretched Mildred will have to die. My soul... oh my soul...! What does batrachians mean?'

> "'I only know,' Eliphas answered, 'that it is a Greek word that means frog.'

> "The servant did not delay in coming with wine and cake, yet the abbot rejected all food. Eliphas took some and tried to take his desperate friend from that lethargy, but it was useless to try to reanimate him. Thus, with his heart in sorrow Eliphas went back to his home.

> "On the following day he went to inquire about the well-being of the abbot and the Duchess.

"Mildred was getting worse continually. The attending physician gave death as his final diagnosis.

"The abbot was also in a serious state; he was refusing any food. In the beginning, he did not respond to the questions of his friend, and stated to him that he thought to end his days by means of starvation. Deeply saddened, Levi left, worrying about the tragic consequences of the sinful invocation.

"During the two following afternoons, Levi sank again into his customary studies and, while reading the *Enquiridion* of Leon III, he stopped in a point in which, by means of the key of Trithemus, the following kabbalistic esoteric writing was deciphered as follows: 'An appreciated maleficent enchantment is the one of the frog.'

We abstain from delivering the secret formula of the toad in order not to give weapons to the perverse criminals of black magic.

"As if lightning crossed the mind of Eliphas, and without even closing the book, he put on a coverall and thrust himself through the streets of London, which was sinking within the vesper twilight. Finally, he found a carriage and the time taken in arriving at the palace of the Duke seemed to him unbearable. Tearful faces received and informed him: 'The Duchess is in agony; the last sacraments are being administered to her...'

"'I can save her,' Eliphas cried out, and separating the astonishing servants, he hurried to the room of Mildred, where he found the Duke. With panting breath, Eliphas beseeched him: "You know me enough in order to know that I am of his confidence. Believe me then, that all hope is not yet lost. Inasmuch as the Duchess lives, there is no need to despair. Thus, I request from you to leave me alone with her, and for God's sake, do not ask me anything... have confidence in me!'

"Although overwhelmed and confused to the extreme, the Duke acceded to the desire of Eliphas, requesting those present in the room—namely, a doctor, a priest, and a maiden of the patient—to leave.

"Once alone, Levi closed the door and came near to the bed of the Princess. 'As I already suspected,' he murmured when seeing Mildred sunk in a form of catalepsy with the eyes blank. Her lips were bluish and she was breathing with a smooth deathly pace.

"Immediately, Levi put his hands to work; thus he began to raise the hardwood floor of the threshold, but the wood resisted his trembling fingers. He removed his knife from the pocket, whose leaf he broke in his frenetic attempt. Finally, and with desperate force, he managed to raise the strip. His fingers were bleeding, but his effort had been useless..... Nothing was hidden there! Then he raised the carpets... but nothing either! He then went back to watch the Duchess, who breathed with difficulty, and observed that her contracted left hand was hanging singularly to one side. 'The bed,' Levi thought. Thus, in the certainty of searching now in the right place, he lifted the patient from her bed and placed her as gently as he could upon an Ottoman that was against the wall.

"Next, he dedicated himself with increasing excitement to remove blankets and pillows... but nothing... nothing. He removed the mattress and opened it; he touched, he felt, enquired within its puffy insides... and... then his fingers encountered a softish, spongy object; he grasped it, removed it... and in fact, that was what he was looking for.

"He rushed outside the room, gave the Duke a brief explanation, asked for an available carraige, and went with extreme speed to his home, where when arriving he placed himself to the task of burning in the flames of fish and sulfur, such an infernal beast, by following exactly the prescription of the *Enquiridión*.

"Right away he opened widely the window of his room, in order for the terrible stench to disappear, and—overwhelmed by enormous fatigue—laid down dressed as he was on his bed, sinking himself into a deep dream."

"The next day, he was received as a savior in the palace of the Duke. In a amazing manner, and in an absolutely incomprehensible manner for the doctors, the state of health of the young Duchess had improved to such a point that a frank overcoming of the crisis was already being spoken of.

"The same day, October 28, 1865, London was impressed with the sensational news that the diva of the ballet Maria Bertin had suddenly passed away without any disease; but this news was not the only one: a few hours later another close relative of the Duke was also snatched by death; she was an old maid who had been an impassioned enemy of Mildred, and who in vain had tried to prevent the marriage of the Duke with the Catholic Princess.

The Mysteries of Life and Death

Chapter One

Death

Beloved disciples, I shall speak to you of the problem of death.

Death is our crown. After death, the soul enters into the Astral Light.

When the hour of death comes, the Angel of Death approaches the deathbed. There is a choir of Angels of Death. This choir is conducted by the planet Saturn. Each Angel of Death carries a book. In this book are the names of all the souls who must depart from the flesh. No one dies a day before his appointed time.

The Angel of Death simply removes the soul from the body. The soul is linked to the body by a fine, heavenly cord of a silvery color. The Angel of Death breaks the cord so that the soul cannot re-enter the body.

After death, souls see the sun just as they used to, the clouds, the stars as always, everything just as before. For a while, the souls of the dead do not believe that they have died. These souls see all the things of the world just as they did before; therefore they do not believe that they have died.

The souls of the dead live in the Astral Light. The Astral Light is the light of all enchantments and magic spells. The Astral Light is related to the air; we eat it, we breathe it, but we can see it only with the eyes of the soul.

Souls see themselves wearing the same clothes that they were wearing in life. Little by little, the consciousness of those souls awakens and they begin to realize that they no longer belong to this material world of flesh and bones.

There exist different secrets in order to converse with the souls of the dead; i.e. place in a room the picture of your deceased beloved, and every night, at midnight, enter the room. Put next to the picture the favorite food that your deceased beloved liked the most; serve the food on the same plates that the deceased used; light a candle and call him/her three times by his name. Then, sit next to the picture and start to meditate personally on the life of the defunct one, his/her history, imagining what he/she was when he/she was alive; until you fall asleep. Every night you can perform the experiment at the same hour, in the same room, and seated on the same chair and in the same place, until you can see, hear, and converse personally with the deceased. What is important is that you are able to fall asleep in the moments in which you are meditating on the life of the defunct. So, in the moment of slumber, the deceased will appear and you can converse with him/her personally.

This is not Spiritism, but practical magic. The important thing is for you to have a lot of faith, patience, and much constancy. If you do not get weary, in the end, one given night, the soul of the beloved one will appear and then you will have the pleasure of conversing with the beloved relative that has departed to the beyond; what is important is to see, hear, touch and perceive him/her.

In the East, there exists a cave where those who want to see Buddha enter in order to invoke him. On a certain occasion, a Chinese man who wanted to see Buddha entered the cave and invoked him, yet the Buddha did not appear; thus the man swore that he would never abandon the cave until the Buddha appeared before him. Thus, the man endured many days desperately calling the Buddha, until finally the Buddha appeared in the middle of the cave filled with light and beauty. Then the Buddha blessed the man, and he left the cave very happy. So, this is the same system of invocation used in order to see the souls of the dead and to converse with them.

Chapter Two

The Evolution of the Disembodied Soul

Between death and new birth, the "good souls" must come unrolled within each one of the planetary auras whose mixtures form that which all books of spiritualism denominate "planes." - Samael Aun Weor, *The Zodiacal Course*

The legend of Zoroaster states, "Everyone whose good deeds exceed his sin by three grams, goes to heaven; everyone whose sin is greater, goes to hell; while he, in whom they are equal, remains in the Hamistikan until the future body or resurrection."

Nowadays, in these times of perversity and crude atheistic materialism, a portion of the disembodied join the submerged mineral kingdom (the Infernal Worlds) after the judgment.

Also, many are the millions who enter a new womb immediately, without having had a good vacation within the Superior Worlds.

Certainly, the selection process exists in all of nature, and few are those who achieve Intermediate Liberation and the Transitional Buddhic State.

The disembodied join Eternity under the influences of the Moon and exit Eternity through the doors of the Moon.

In the lesson of Cancer we taught that the entire life of all people is processed under the influences of the Moon, Mercury, Venus, the

Sun, Mars, Jupiter and Saturn; life closes with a Lunar end.

Really, the Moon takes us and the Moon brings us as well. The seven types of planetary vibrations (in their indicated classical order) also repeat themselves after death for, "As it is above, so is it below."

The Essences who, after having been judged have the right to Intermediate Liberation and the Transitional Buddhic State, need a certain type of very special ecstasy and constant Right Effort in order to become liberated, to escape from the Lunar Bodies and the ego.

Fortunately, different groups of Masters assist the disembodied and help them in this work with the Rays of Grace.

In the same manner that republics, kingdoms, presidents, kings, governors, etc. exist in this Cellular World in which we live, likewise in the Molecular World, there are many paradises, regions, and kingdoms where Essences enjoy indescribable states of happiness. - Samael Aun Weor, "Capricorn," *The Esoteric Treatise of Hermetic Astrology*

The souls of the dead in the Astral Plane have to cross the Astral spheres of the Moon, Mercury, Venus, the Sun, Mars, Jupiter, and Saturn. Each one of these planets is wrapped in an Astral atmosphere.

Astral atmospheres penetrate and interpenetrate one another without blending. All these atmospheres are related to the air we breathe.

The Moon

When the soul enters the lunar sphere, it feels strongly drawn toward the place where the body is buried, and it wants to act exactly as if it had flesh and bones. These souls sit down to have meals in their homes and feel the same physical needs as before.

Mercury

When the soul enters the atmosphere of Mercury, it sees that the atmosphere is becoming clearer for it and all things appear even more beautiful to it than before. Those souls who in life were never able to adapt to all the circumstances of existence then suffer unspeakably. Those souls full of pride and haughtiness suffer because they want everybody to respect them, as in the past, for their money and lineage. But in the sphere of Mercury, souls are respected only for their saintliness and their wisdom. Souls which in life were humble, pious, and charitable feel happy in the sphere of Mercury.

Venus

Later on, the soul enters the sphere of Venus. In this sphere, souls again become child-like, and enjoy things as children do, playing in nature's bosom.

In the sphere of Venus, we again become deeply religious and understand that all the religions of the world are pearls strung on the golden thread of divinity. In the sphere of Venus we again become mystical and find delight in nature's woods and mountains. We are happy.

Those souls who never had any kind of religion—materialistic souls—feel out of place there, like chickens in an unfamiliar barnyard. They suffer unspeakably. Those who were delirious and fanatical about religious matters feel immense remorse for their evil deeds because they understand the harm which they did to others. They suffer unspeakably.

Some time afterwards, the soul enters the Solar atmosphere.

The Sun

In this atmosphere, we understand the oneness of lives; we understand that the life which throbs within the heart is the same life that throbs within the very heart of each world that it remembers throughout space. In the sphere of the Sun, we understand what universal brotherhood is, and we feel that we are a single great human family.

Those souls who were selfish experience deep remorse here in the Solar sphere, and great moral suffering. Those souls suffer the remorse for their evil deeds. In the Solar sphere, we see a brother in every face.

Mars

Later on, the soul enters the Martian sphere. In this sphere, we feel the longing to separate ourselves forever from the things of the material world. In this sphere, we lead a life of mystical enchantment, and we feel the strong influence of Francis of Assisi, of Buddha. Here we feel that the life of each flower is our life. Then, we long to withdraw from the material world forever.

Jupiter

Later, the soul enters the sphere of Jupiter. In this sphere, we understand that the religion we had on Earth was only a school which we had to go through. Here, we give up that earthly religion, and then we enter into cosmic consciousness.

Saturn

In this life, the soul becomes submerged much later in the sphere of Saturn and then floats delightedly among all the stars in space. It visits distant worlds and is submerged in an infinity full of indescribable music, of delightful orchestras which resound within the immense chorale of eternity, where only the true happiness of limitless space reigns.

"When the soul wishes to return to that school of
life to perfect itself, when the soul wants to return
to the world, then the Angels of Destiny take that
soul away to a new home."

Chapter Three

Reincarnation and Karma

Within the bosom of infinity, the soul sees thousands of indescribable beings or Angels, Archangels, Thrones, Virtues, Powers, etc., and then it understands that those divine beings were people who perfected themselves and who suffered greatly in the school of life.

The soul understands that life is a school, and it wishes to return to that school to perfect itself. When the soul wishes to return to that school of life to perfect itself, when the soul wants to return to the world, then the Angels of Destiny take that soul away to a new home. The Angels of Destiny unite with the soul or, we should say, connect the soul with the spermatozoon of the father's semen. This spermatozoon—chosen by the soul who is going to be born—fertilizes the womb. The soul stays within the maternal womb for nine months, forming its new physical body.

The soul is not a prisoner, however, for it can enter and leave the maternal womb and its body at will. After nine months, the soul is born with a new child's body.

If in the previous reincarnation we did much evil, then in the following one it is our turn to suffer the consequences, and we are born with very bad luck. Our business deals fail, misery pursues us, and we suffer immensely. If previously we had taken away another man's wife, then ours is now taken from us. If we were bad parents, if we did not know how to treat our children well, then it is our lot to be born into a place more bitter than bile. Our parents will make us suffer the same way that we made our children suffer in the previous reincarnation. He who sows thunderbolts has no choice but to reap storms. Let him who sows corn eat his corn. Each person reaps what he sows.

If God sends a soul that has done no good to be born in comfortable surroundings and souls who have done no evil to be born into misery, where would God's justice be?

A genius becomes a genius because in millions of lives he has struggled to achieve perfection. We are the result of our previous reincarnations. With the yard-stick with which you measure, you will be measured.

There are forty-two Masters of Karma.

Karma is the Law of Compensation.

In each reincarnation, we should strive to be more and more perfect. We have come into this world millions of times, and it is our lot to keep returning until we become perfect.

There is a system for remembering our past reincarnations: this system is the retrospective exercise. The disciple lies in his bed every night, and then practices retrospective exercises. The disciple begins by remembering everything that happened one hour before he went to bed, two hours before, every moment of the afternoon and the morning throughout the day. The disciple makes an effort to remember everything from yesterday and the day before. One must do the effort of remembering everything that happened during one month, two months, three months, one year, ten years, twenty years behind, until minutely remembering the entire history of his life.

The disciple must make the effort to remember the first five years of his life. The disciple will notice that this is very difficult. The first five years of life are very difficult to remember, however there exists a secret to remember this: the disciple must fall asleep while mentally pronouncing the following mantras:

Raaaaaa Oooommmm Gaaaaaa Ooooommmm...

The disciple will slumber while pronouncing mentally these two words, and will make the effort to remember in his sleepy state everything that happened to him during the first five years of the history of his infancy. These manners of dreams are truthful.

Our disciples must open the Bible and study the book of Daniel so that they can learn about this.

After our disciples have remembered their present entire life, then they must make the effort to remember the last moments of their past reincarnation. If the disciple, while performing this practice, quietly falls asleep, then on any given coming date, during sleep, he might remember his entire past reincarnation. With this secret, any disciple can not only remember his past reincarnation, but moreover, he/she can remember all of their past reincarnations. What is necessary is to practice every night with a lot of faith until attaining triumph.

ANUBIS WEARING HIS JACKAL MASK OFFICIATES IN THE JOURNEY OF THE DEAD.

Chapter Four
Karma

In the inner worlds, there is a temple where the forty-two Judges of Karma officiate. They are the forty-two jackals. They are named as such because they cover their heads with a kind of religious mask shaped like the head of a wolf dog or jackal. These forty-two Masters are the masters of the Law of Compensation: the Law of Karma.

Everything evil that we do to others in past reincarnations we must pay for in the following incarnation.

One pays Karma not only for the evil one does, but also for the good that one fails to do when able to do it. He who has the means with which to pay, pays and comes out well in his dealings. He, who does not have the means to pay, undoubtedly must pay with inevitable pain.

The Lords of Karma say:

"Do good deeds so as to pay your debts."

"The lion of the law is combatted with the scale."

If the plate containing bad deeds weighs more, then we can put good deeds in the other plate.

The saying goes: increase the weight of the plate containing good deeds to make it tip in your favor. This is how we can cancel old debts and avoid grief for ourselves. When an inferior law is transcended by a superior law, the superior law erases the inferior law.

Our disciples must learn to travel in the Astral Body to visit the temple of the Lords of Karma. The chief of this temple is **Anubis**.

The key to traveling in the Astral Body is very simple: the disciple should lie in his bed and try to go to sleep calmly. Then the disciple should get up from his bed while he is slumbering, and leave his room. If the disciple jumps slightly, intending to stay afloat in the air, he will see with astonishment that he is delightfully floating in the air and that he can travel with the

Astral Body to any place on Earth. The disciple can go with the Astral Body to the palace of the Lords of Karma. In this temple, he can settle his affairs with the Lords of Karma. When we say affairs, we refer to our outstanding debts to cosmic justice. The Lords of the Law also grant credit, but all credit must be paid back by doing good works for the benefit of humanity. We must learn to go out in the Astral Body to settle our affairs personally with the Lords of Karma. When a man learns to manage his accounts, he can guide his life better.

Chapter Five

The Innermost

Saint Paul said:

> *Know ye not that ye are the temple of God, and that*
> *the Spirit of God dwelleth in you?* - 1 Corinthians 3:16

The "Spirit of God" is our Divine Spirit; it is the Innermost. Thus, the Innermost is the most divine thing that we have within ourselves. It is God among us. The Innermost is beautiful, sublime, pure.

The Innermost has two things: the soul and the body. The soul is in contact with the sympathetic nervous system. The Innermost is in contact with the cerebrospinal system; that is, with the cerebrospinal column.

The soul suffers, enjoys itself, works, acquires experience, commits errors, is imperfect. The soul is sinful. The soul lets itself be carried away by passions, and suffers for this. Thus, if the soul wishes to become an Angel again, it has no choice but to put a stop to its defects, to become pure again, to purify itself, to cleanse itself to achieve unity with the Innermost.

When the soul merges with the Innermost, that is, mingles with the Innermost, when it again becomes one with Him, then it becomes an Angel. The Innermost is a flame. The soul is another flame.

When the two flames join, they form a single flame. This flame is an Angel. And thus, Angels are perfect people, repentant souls, people who repented their sins, their evil deeds, their fornications, their acts of adultery, their homicides, etc.

God is the Innermost Spirit who is within us, the universal spirit of life. He is the divine fire which is in the rock, in the waters, in the air, everywhere in space. All infinity is animated by divine fire. God is a sea of burning fire. The burning fire is everywhere. Fire is God. Fire is Pentecost. It is God. The fire that Moses saw in the bush of Horeb is God. The Innermost that we have within ourselves is a flame of divine fire: it is God within us.

The Innermost is the divine person. It is the heavenly person who is within us. When the soul mingles with the Innermost, it becomes Him. Then we become Angels. Angels are in nature, they are in the rivers, in the sea, in the clouds, in the volcanoes, everywhere.

Chapter Six
Sexual Magic

We left Eden through the gates of sex. Eden is sex itself.

We can only re-enter Eden through the gate we left through. This gate is sex. No one can enter Paradise through the wrong gate or gates. They do not exist in Paradise.

Paradise has no such gates. We must enter the same way we left. Eden is sex itself.

Sexual forces are everywhere; everything that exists in the world is the child of sex. We ourselves exist in the world because we had a father and a mother.

In Eden, there are two Trees: the Tree of Knowledge of Good and Evil, and the Tree of Life.

We left Eden for having eaten the forbidden fruit. We cannot enter Eden so long as we continue eating this fruit.

At the base of the spinal column there is a bone called the coccyx; in this bone there is an ethereal center called Muladhara, and within this ethereal center there is an inlaid serpent of fire. This serpent is the fire of the Pentecost, the fire of the Holy Spirit. This fire is terrific; it has tremendous power. This is the igneous serpent of our magical powers. In India, this serpent is called the Kundalini.

The wise men of India awaken Kundalini with Sexual Magic. Sexual Magic is very easy: a man and a woman may sexually unite and become "one flesh." Both, however, men and women, must withdraw from the sexual act before and without spilling the seminal liquor [through the orgasm]. The seminal liquor must not be spilled within the womb; moreover, the seed must not be allowed to spill outside that organ. The man must withdraw from the woman, and the woman from the man, restraining the sexual impulse to avoid spilling the seminal liquor.

By restraining the sexual impulse, the semen [sexual energy] is turned into very subtle energies that rise up to the brain through two delicate nerve cords. These cords are the two witnesses which we are told about in the Apocalypse. They are the two olive branches of the temple, the two candlesticks that stand before the throne of the God of Earth.

A Yogi makes his home without needing to break the sixth commandment of the Law of God:

Thou shalt not fornicate.

During the act of sexual magic, it is possible for a spermatozoon, which the lunar hierarchies use to fertilize the womb, to escape, without there being any need to spill the semen.

God is the Innermost, and his throne is the spinal column. Sexual forces are solar and lunar. When the solar and lunar atoms unite in the coccyx, then the igneous snake of our magical powers awakens. With this snake we can awaken all the powers of the wise men.

This serpent enters through the lower orifice of the spinal cord. The cord is hollow inside. Along the spinal cord there is a canal through which the sacred fire of the Holy Spirit rises upward, little by little, until it reaches the brain. When the igneous serpent reaches the brain, then the soul is united with the Innermost and thus enters Eden.

The soul who unites with the Innermost has power over earth, over water, over fire. It can command winds and hurricanes. It can hear and see the things of the heavens, of the Earth and the abyss, and is able to know all divine things.

Jesus Christ said:

> *Verily, verily, I say to you, the one believing in me will also do the works that I do; and greater works than these will he do.* - John 14:12

...and so the only way to enter Paradise is through the gate through which we left it. That gate is sex. Nobody can enter Paradise through false gates.

Single people must transmute the seminal liquor with deep breathing, keeping the lungs full thirty seconds or more. This Swara exercise must be performed daily.

Chapter Seven

The Seven Churches

The seven churches mentioned in the Apocalypse of Saint John are not on the Asian continent as is presumed by the ignorant. They are in the spinal column.

The Apocalypse of Saint John is a book sealed with seven seals. The book is Man itself. No one except the Lamb, the Innermost who lies within us, can open this book and remove the seven seals.

The seven churches are seven nerve centers in the spinal column.

Ephesus

The first church is the church of Ephesus. It is located in the coccygeal cavity. Within it is the sacred serpent, the metal snake, the bronze serpent that healed the Israelites in the desert.

When this church is opened, we acquire power over volcanoes and earthquakes and over the creatures that live under the ground.

Smyrna

When the serpent reaches the prostate, it awakens the second church of Smyrna, and we acquire power over water and storms.

Pergamos

When the sacred serpent rises in the central channel of the spinal column to the level of the navel, the third church, the church of Pergamos, is awakened. We then acquire power over lightning, fire, and erupting volcanoes. We can command

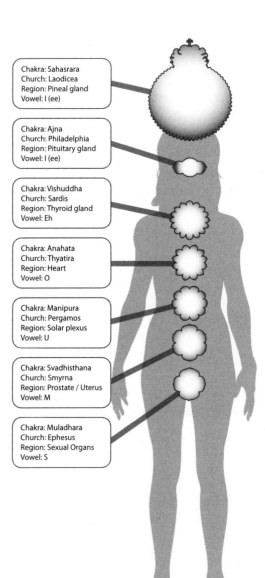

Chakra: Sahasrara
Church: Laodicea
Region: Pineal gland
Vowel: I (ee)

Chakra: Ajna
Church: Philadelphia
Region: Pituitary gland
Vowel: I (ee)

Chakra: Vishuddha
Church: Sardis
Region: Thyroid gland
Vowel: Eh

Chakra: Anahata
Church: Thyatira
Region: Heart
Vowel: O

Chakra: Manipura
Church: Pergamos
Region: Solar plexus
Vowel: U

Chakra: Svadhisthana
Church: Smyrna
Region: Prostate / Uterus
Vowel: M

Chakra: Muladhara
Church: Ephesus
Region: Sexual Organs
Vowel: S

THE SEVEN CHURCHES / CHAKRAS

volcanoes, and they obey us. We can command fire, and the universal fire obeys us.

Thyatira

When the snake reaches the heart, the church of Thyatira is awakened. This church gives us power over cyclones, over the wind, and over hurricanes.

Sardis

When the sacred snake reaches the level of the throat, we can hear the speech of the Angels, the words of the souls of the dead, etc. This is the church of Sardis.

Philadelphia

When the sacred snake rises through the spinal column and reaches as high as the brow, then we can see things of the other world: the Astral Light, the souls of the dead, Archangels, Seraphim, Powers, Virtues, Thrones, etc. This is the church of Philadelphia.

Laodicea

When the snake reaches the upper part of the cranium, the church of Laodicea opens. This is the diamond eye. He who opens this eye knows all the things of heaven and earth. He becomes tremendous. He sees everywhere; he is unaware of nothing. After this, the soul unites with the Innermost and becomes a master, prophet, wise man, enlightened being, possessor of power. He sees all, hears all, is ignorant of nothing.

Once the soul has united totally, absolutely with the Innermost, then it becomes an Angel. Angels are perfected people.

Daniel prays to God as Nebuchadnezzar arrives for the interpretation

Chapter Eight

Astral Voyages

The soul is enshrouded in a fluidic body called the Astral Body. The Astral Body is similar to the physical body. Within the Astral Body is the soul with its mind, with its will, with its conscience, with its feelings. Thus, the Astral Body is marvelous; this is the soul's body.

When the flesh and bone body is asleep, the soul leaves the flesh and bone body and wanders all over. The soul voyages in its Astral Body.

When King Nebuchadnezzar lay sleeping in his bed, he thought about what he would be in the future; then he fell asleep. The King's soul then left the flesh and bone body, traveled in the Astral Plane, and saw a statue whose head was of gold, its breast and arms were of silver, its legs were of iron, and its feet were partly iron and partly baked clay.

The King ordered all wise men, astrologers, and Chaldean soothsayers to be called forth so that they could prophesy the dream of the statue for him and give their statement. No one was capable of telling the King about his dream, for he did not want to tell it to anyone. On account of this the wise men went to their death.

The prophet Daniel went to his house and prayed to the Lord Jehovah with his companions, and then went to bed and slept peacefully.

Daniel's soul then left his body, and saw in the Astral World King Nebuchadnezzar's famous statue.

The next day Daniel went before the King and prophesied the dream of the statue for him, and gave him his statement, that is, the interpretation. The King was astounded, and honors were heaped upon Daniel.

And so, dreams are astral experiences. Our disciples must call them astral experiences and not dreams. Our disciples must say, "Last night I was at such and such a place; last night I was in the Astral Body at such and such a place; I had an experience with so-and-so in such-and-such a temple, etc."

In the Astral Body, we Masters subject disciples to many tests. In the Astral Plane and in Astral Bodies, our disciples receive their initiations in the temples of the Astral Plane.

The Astral Plane is known in the Bible by the name of "Mount." On the Mount, Jesus transfigured himself before his disciples. The Mount is Astral.

During sleep, our disciples are on the Mount. It is in the interest of our disciples to study the Book of Daniel in the Bible. All of Daniel's visions were on the Mount, on the Astral Plane, and not on the physical plane.

Our disciples, upon awakening from their material sleep, must not move, because with the body's movement the Astral Body is stirred, and recollections are lost. Upon awakening, disciples must make an effort to remember all those places where they were while their bodies were sleeping. They must make an effort to remember all their past experiences on the Astral Plane. Our disciples must not recount their experiences to anyone.

The Book of the Dead

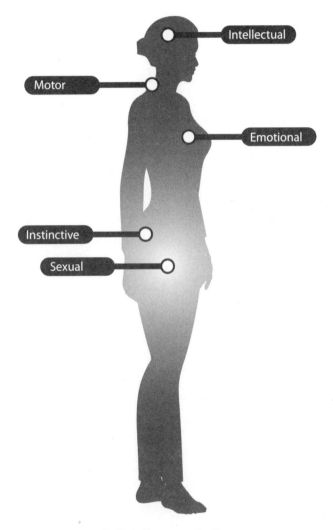

THE THREE BRAINS AND THE FIVE CENTERS

The motor, instinctive, and sexual centers can be grouped
together as one "brain" or arena of functionality.

Chapter One
Death

During the course of existence, different types of energies flow through the human organism.

Each type of energy has its own system of action. Each type of energy manifests itself in its own time.

The motor and muscular force manifests itself four and a half months after conception; this is related to the birth of the respiratory and pulmonary function. At ten and a half months growth occurs with all its marvellous metabolisms and conjunctive tissues. When the child is between two and three years old, the fontanel of the newly born closes and the cerebro-spinal system is completely formed.

The human personality is formed during the first seven years, and at fourteen years personal energy appears and, flowing domineeringly through the sympathetic nervous system, sex appears at thirty-five years in its transcendental form as creative emotion. It is upon reaching this age that we can make what is called Soul. The common man does not have a soul, or rather, he still is not a true man; he doesn't even have a soul.

The intellectual animal falsely named "man" is a machine controlled by the legion of the ego. This is pluralized. "I must read a book," says the intellectual function. "I am going to a football match," says the motor function; "I am hungry, I shall not go anywhere," states the digestion; "I prefer to find a woman," says the ego of passion etc. etc. All these egos argue amongst themselves. The ego that today swears faithfulness to Gnosis is replaced by another that hates Gnosis. The ego that today adores a woman is later replaced by another that hates her. Only by making the Soul do we establish a permanent principle of consciousness within ourselves.

He who has Soul lives consciously after death. The Soul may be created with the accumulation of the finest energies the organism produces and the crystallization through supreme efforts, to make one Self-conscious in a total and definitive way. Unfortunately, the intellectual animal called man wastes these energies stupidly on cravings, anger, fears, hate, envy, passions, jealousy, etc.

It is urgent that we create conscious will; it is indispensable that we subject all our thoughts and acts to inner judgment. Only in this way can we know ourselves in depth in order to create the Soul.

The Ray of Death

The Ray of Death reduces so-called man to a simple molecular quintessence, in the same way that a ton of flowers may be reduced to a single drop of essential perfume. Because the energy of death is so strong, it destroys the human organism totally. It is a current of such high voltage that it inevitably destroys the organism when it travels through it. As a flash of lightning can tear a tree apart, so the ray of death reduces the human body to ashes. It is the only type of energy that the body cannot resist.

This ray connects death with conception. The two extremes meet. When the essence is detached from the old body on the terrible impact of the ray of death, a tremendous electrical tension is produced on a key note, the axiomatic result of which is the movement and combination of the determining genes of the future physical body. This is how the fine constituents of a fertilized egg are arranged in the corresponding order, having electrical tension and the key note of death for a basis.

What Continues

Two things go to the grave. The first is the physical body, and the second is the human personality. As we have already said, the latter is formed during the first seven years of infancy and is strengthened with experiences. Sometimes the personality wanders through the cemetery, or leaves its grave when the mourners visit and bring flowers. But the personality soon disintegrates. The personality is energetic and atomic. The personality is perishable. There is no future for the personality of a dead person, it is mortal.

The personality is not re-incarnated. The personality is a child of its time and dies in its time. What continues is the essence, that is to say, the phantom of the dead person. Within the phantom, the reincarnating ego, the self, is found. This is the legion of devils, which is what continues to exist.

It is a mistake to divide ourselves between two egos, one a superior sort and the other inferior: The ego is a legion of devils, which normally develops within us; that is all.

A lot is said in occultist literature about a superior ego, about a divine ego, but in fact the so-called superior ego is not an ego. The Divine Being transcends an ego-ism. That which does not have a profane name is the Being, the Innermost.

The Essence, within the molecular phantom of the dead, normally lives in the Molecular World. On dying, we leave the Cellular World and enter the Molecular World; in the Molecular World we use a molecular body.

The Tibetan "Book of the Dead" (the Bardo Thodol) says the following:

> Oh! Noble by birth... your present body being a body
> of desire... is not a body of gross material, so now you
> have the power to pass through any mass of rocks,
> hills, boulders, earth, houses, and Mount Meru itself,
> without meeting any obstacle... you now possess the
> power of miraculous actions, which is not the fruit
> of any samadhi, but the power which comes to you
> naturally... You can instantaneously be in any place
> you want; you have the power to get there in the time
> it takes a man to open and shut his hand. Do not
> desire the various powers of illusion or of changing
> form, do not desire them.

The Vital Body

In the human organism, there is a thermoelectrical, magnetic body. This is the vital body. This body is the seat of organic

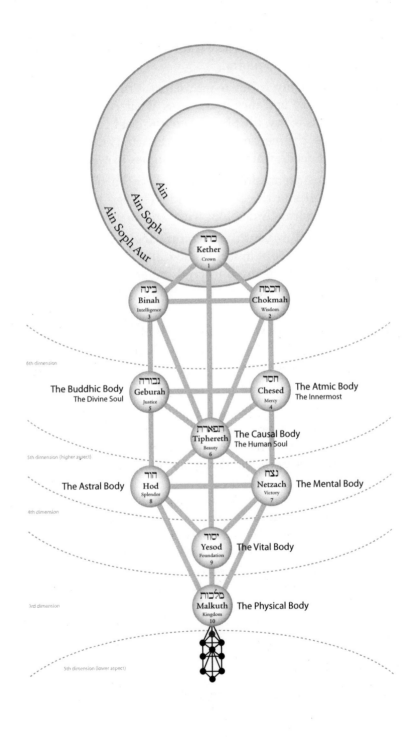

Ain

Ain Soph

Ain Soph Aur

כתר
Kether
Crown
1

בינה
Binah
Intelligence
3

חכמה
Chokmah
Wisdom
2

6th dimension

The Buddhic Body
The Divine Soul

נבורה
Geburah
Justice
5

חסד
Chesed
Mercy
4

The Atmic Body
The Innermost

תפארת
Tiphereth
Beauty
6

The Causal Body
The Human Soul

5th dimension (higher aspect)

The Astral Body

הוד
Hod
Splendor
8

נצח
Netzach
Victory
7

The Mental Body

4th dimension

יסוד
Yesod
Foundation
9

The Vital Body

3rd dimension

מלכות
Malkuth
Kingdom
10

The Physical Body

5th dimension (lower aspect)

life. No organism could live without the vital body. Each atom of the vital body enters into each atom of the physical body, to make it vibrate intensely. All chemical, physiological, and biological phenomena, all phenomena of perception, all metabolic processes, all action of calories etc. have their basis in the vital body. In fact, this body is the superior section of the physical body, the tetra-dimensional body.

In the last instant of life, this body escapes from the physical organism. The vital body does not enter the grave. The vital body floats near the grave and disintegrates slowly as the corpse disintegrates. Only the corpse and the personality of the dead man go to the grave.

The vital body has more reality than the physical body. We know very well that the physical body changes totally every seven years and not a single old atom remains in the body. But the vital body does not change. Contained in this body are all the atoms of childhood, adolescence, youth, maturity, old age, and decrepitude.

The physical body belongs to the world of three dimensions. The vital body is the body of the fourth dimension.

The Fifth Dimension

The ghosts of the dead live in the fifth dimension; this is eternity. Length, width, and depth are the three dimensions of the cellular world. Time is the fourth dimension; eternity, the fifth dimension, and that which is beyond eternity and time corresponds to the sixth dimension.

In fact, liberation begins in the sixth dimension, the world of the divine Spirit; it is the Electronic World of the sixth dimension. All those who die enter the fifth dimension.

Eternity opens to devour the dead and then expels them from its bosom to return them to the world of time and physical form. The dead are expelled from eternity because they still do not have Being. Only those who have Being can live in eternity. The Being is the Innermost, the Spirit. It is necessary to work first with molecular material to make Soul, and then to refine the energy of this Soul to a higher grade to make Spirit. It is necessary to transmute molecular material into electronic material and cause the fission of the atom to liberate the sacred fire that converts us into divine Spirits.

Chapter Two
The Angels of Death

Contemporary positivist philosophy is based on the existence of matter (materialism) and energy. There have been many arguments about force and matter, but these latter continue in spite of all speculations of "x, y, and unknown." The revolutionary followers of positivist philosophy are always trying to define one through the other; it is ridiculous—extremely ridiculous—to define the unknown through the unknown. Materialist philosophy says, "Matter is that through which changes called movements are effected, and movements are those changes which are effected in matter." This is the identity of the unknown: x = y; y = x. In total: ignorance, a vicious, absurd circle.

In fact, no one has seen either matter or energy. Human beings only perceive phenomena, things, forms, images etc. We have never seen the substance of things. The given substance is not solely matter, but wood, copper, tin, stone, etc.; nor have we ever seen energy separated from movement. We have never seen matter separated from forms and objects.

A handful of earth has a defined form; a statue has a defined form; the planet Earth has a defined form, etc. etc. In fact, so-called matter is only a concept as abstract as beauty, goodness, value, work, etc.; no one is able to see the substance itself of things. No one knows the "thing itself."

We see the physical image of man, but we do not see the thing itself, the body of the man. Only by developing the spatial sense can we see the body itself, the thing itself.

Space is the vehicle of the mind, and only with the sense of space can we know the thing itself, which is a man's vital body. What would be the "thing itself" of a plant? It's vital body. What would be the "thing itself" of an animal? The animal's vital body. What would be the "thing itself" of the Earth? The vital Earth. The vital Earth represents the Earth in itself. The life of organisms depends on this vital Earth. The vital Earth is found in the fourth dimension.

A point in movement leaves a trace: this is the line. A line in movement leaves a trace: this is the surface. A surface in movement is converted into a solid, and a solid in movement is converted into a hyper-solid. In fact, the hyper-solid is the thing itself; the hyper-solid belongs to the fourth dimension. We can only see hyper-solids with the spatial sense. In fact, the temporal sense is only the surface of the spatial sense.

Upon leaving itself, the point is converted into a line. When the line leaves itself, it is converted into a solid. The solid, leaving itself with a movement in space, is converted into a hyper-solid. Hyper-solids are contained within solid bodies. If the vital body moves to the outside of an organism, the organism inevitably disintegrates.

The vital body belongs to the fourth dimension and the human essence to the fifth dimension. The Angels who govern the processes of conception normally live in the fourth dimension, and those who govern death, in the fifth dimension. The first connect the ego to the zoosperm; the second break the connection that exists between the ego and the physical body.

The Angels of Death are in themselves perfect men. The loss of a loved one is very bitter and it might seem that the Angels of Death are too cruel, but in fact they are not, even though this may seem incredible. The Angels of Death work according to Laws, with supreme wisdom and great love and charity. We can only understand this clearly when we identify them in the Molecular World and in the Electronic World.

The Angels of Life give a human being a vital body so that he may live. The Angels of Death take life from a human being. They do this by cutting the "silver cord." This cord corresponds to the umbilical cord, and it is sevenfold in its inner constitution. The Angels of Life connect the molecular body of the disincarnated person with the zoosperm, so that it acquires a new body. In fact, the silver cord is the thread of life that the Angels of Death break on the appropriate day and at the right time, in accordance with the Law of Destiny. This marvellous thread belongs to the superior dimensions of space and can only be seen with the spatial sense.

The dying often see the Angel of Death as a quite horrible skeletal figure. In fact, what happens is that he dresses in the clothes that suit his job. In practical life, the policeman wears his uniform, the doctor his white coat, the judge his gown, the priest his habit, etc. The funereal clothes and the skeletal figure of the Angels of Death horrify those who still have not awakened consciousness. The funereal symbols of the Angels of Death are the sickle that cuts down life, the skull of death, the long-eared owl, etc. Outside their work, the appearance of the Angels of Death is that of beautiful children, sublime maidens, venerable Masters, etc.

The Angels of Death are graded in the form of hierarchies. There are grades and levels among them. The Angels of Death have their temples in the Molecular World; they also have their grades, and their palaces and libraries. There in the immensity of the great ocean of life, there exists a funereal palace where one of the imperial Genies of death has its dwelling place; its face is that of an ineffable maiden and its body like that of a man. This marvellous being is totally androgynous. This marvellous being is a divine hermaphrodite. Thousands of Angels of Death work under its direction. In its library, there are thousands of molecular volumes where the Karmic names and dates of all those who must die are written, each with its own day and time according to the Law of Destiny. The science of death is terribly divine.

The intellectual animal falsely named man dies unconsciously and is born unconsciously, and goes blindly from the cradle to the grave, without knowing where he comes from or where he is going. By creating the Soul, we awaken the consciousness, and only then become aware of the mysteries of life and death.

Any man with Soul can negotiate with the Angels of Death and disincarnate himself at will, in accordance with his needs. This means having the power to lengthen his life if he considers it necessary in order to Realize or complete some task in the physical world.

Those who have transfigured themselves in the Electronic World, those who have an electronic body because they have made Soul, can command the Angels of Death and keep their physical body for millions of years. These are the great saviors of humanity; the great Rectors of the world. Let us remember the King of the world cited by Ferdinand Ossendowski in his book entitled "Beasts, Men, and Gods." This great Being lives in Agharti and has a body of indecipherable age. Extremely old religious writings mention this great being. Let us remember Sanat Kumara, the Ancient of Days, the great immolate, the founder of the College of Initiates of the great White Lodge. This adept lives in the Gobi desert in an isolated oasis. The body of this great Being is more than 18 million years old. With him, in the same oasis, live a group of adepts with immortal Lemurian bodies. All these adepts travel through the superior dimensions of space with their physical bodies. They have the power to tele-transport themselves with their physical bodies through the fourth or fifth dimensions. They all exercise power over the Angels of Death. They are the adepts of the mysteries of life and death. They have all had to work with the Great Arcanum.

Chapter Three

The Tribunals of Karma

The Tibetan "Book of the Dead" (Bardo Thodol) says:

*You have been unconscious for the last three and
a half days. As soon as you recover you will have
consciousness...*

What happened? Well, at this moment all Samsara (the phenomenal universe) is in revolution. Admission to the Electronic and Molecular Worlds at the moment of death is a tremendous test for man's consciousness. The Tibetan "Book of the Dead" states that at the moment of death all men fall into a faint that lasts three and a half days. Max Heindel, Rudolf Steiner, and many other authors sustain that in these three and a half days the disincarnate ego sees its whole life pass in the form of images, in retrospective order. The said authors state that these memories are contained in the vital body. This is true, but it is only a part of the truth. The images and memories contained in the vital body and its retrospective vision is only an automatic repetition of something similar in the Electronic World.

At the moment of death and during the three and a half days following death, our consciousness and inner judgment are liberated by an electronic discharge. We then see our whole life pass in a retrospective form. The discharge is so strong that it makes a person fall into a state of coma and incoherent dreams. Only those who possess what is called Soul can resist the electronic discharge without losing consciousness.

When the three and a half days have passed, the Essence enters a state of Lunar-type consciousness. At the moment of death we re-live our life in a retrospective form, under electronic discharge, but in a very rapid and terrible way; in the Molecular World we again re-live the life that has just passed, but in much slower form, because time in the Molecular World is slower than in the Electronic World.

Under the Lunar influence, we re-live our life from old age to childhood and birth. Then the disincarnate visit all those places in which they related. They re-live each scene of their life, saying and doing the same as they did in life, feeling joy for the good works and profound moral pain for the bad.

It is clear that when the retrospective work is finished, we have full awareness of the final result of the life that has just passed. It is then, and only then, that all those who are not definitively lost make the decision to correct their errors and pay their debts. Only those who are completely lost do not respond to the terrible impact of the Molecular and Electronic Worlds. In fact, those beings are already so materialized that they return to the mineral world. This is the Christian hell, Ammit, the Egyptian monster, devourer of the dead, with its giant crocodile jaws, the devourer of hearts, the cosmic vultures that consume the waste and left-overs of humanity, the Roman Avernus, the Hindustan Avitchi, etc.

All the planes of existence mentioned by Theosophy may be perfectly synthesized in four regions: Hell, Earth, Paradise, and Heaven. That is to say: Mineral World, Cellular World, Molecular World and Electronic World.

The Final Judgment is what decides the fate of the disincarnate. When the retrospective work is finished, we have to present ourselves before the Tribunals of Karma. In these tribunals we have to answer charges. The ruling of the Judges is definitive. It is incorrect to say that all beings pass to the regions of Paradise or to celestial-type states of happiness after Judgment. In fact, only a very small minority of beings pass to the ineffable regions mentioned by Theosophy. The Final Judgment divides the disincarnate into three groups:

1. Those who return immediately;

2. Those who rise to paradisiacal and celestial states and return much later;

3. Those who enter the mineral kingdom (Hell).

Chapter Four

The Four Circles

Our solar system is a complete body with four complete circles. The circumference of the each of the circles has its respective time pattern.

The circle of the mineral region called Hell or Avitchi etc. has a time scale that goes from 80,000,000 to 80 years; a terribly slow time, very appropriate for all the mineral processes which take place within the earthly crust in that kingdom called Hell or Avitchi.

The circle of cellular life extends from 60 years to a month, and within this time all organisms that live on the surface of the earth normally develop.

The circle of molecular life extends from one month to 40 minutes and measures all phenomena and happenings of the Molecular World. The Molecular World is the region or regions of the atmosphere, the Paradise of all religions.

The circle of electronic life oscillates between 40 and 2.5 seconds. This is the time of the celestial regions with which the phenomena of light and solar happenings are measured.

Avitchi

The infernal region of Avitchi is within the mineral crust of the earth. Avitchi is below the limits of external sensory perception. Avitchi belongs to the densest mineral regions. Avitchi could never be discovered with the physical senses because it belongs to the Ultra.

Avitchi has seven terribly dense regions. Avitchi is symbolized by the infernos of the great religions. Inferno derives from "infernus," lower region, the atomic infernos of nature. These are the submerged worlds, within the earth's interior.

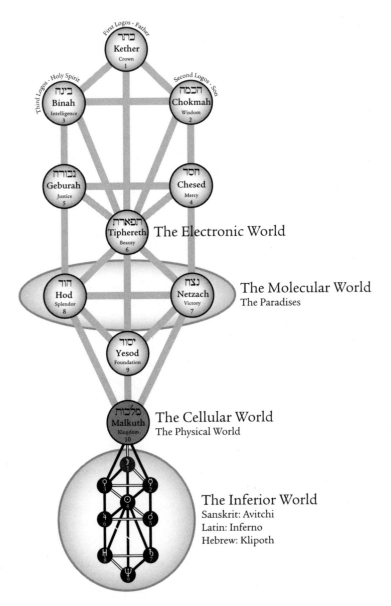

THE FOUR CIRCLES AND THEIR RELATIONSHIP TO THE TREE OF LIFE

When a human being has become too materialistic, too lazy, then after judgment he enters Avitchi. The Tibetan "Book of the Dead" says:

On falling there, you will have to suffer unbearably,
where there is certainly no chance to escape.

Those who become more and more evil enter the kingdom with which they have more affinity. This is the kingdom of rocks where the petrified fossil remains of those who were once living creatures abide. These are the people with hearts of stone, hearts of flint, etc. These people no longer respond to any kind of punishment, and each time that they return all they do is work in evil and for evil. They love evil for evil's sake. Because of their persistence in crime, because of their exaggerated materialism, they have become, in some way, mineral. This is the melting pot, the aim of which is to liberate a fraction of the causal particle, the prime material, the psychic product, a type of embryo soul shut up in the diabolical, mineralized host.

In Avitchi, those who are lost are devoluted in time. From the human state, they devolve to the animal state, then they return to the plant kingdom and lastly to the mineral. Afterwards, they disintegrate, are reduced to cosmic dust. When these shadowy entities disintegrate, something escapes inwards and upwards. What escapes is the embryo of the Soul, the prime material that returns to the world of the Spirit.

Let us remember the vision of Er, who says:

And he said as they arrived, all returned joyfully
to the meadows and camped there as if in a
congregation... and they talked among themselves
- some moaning and crying, when they remember
the terrible things that they had suffered and seen
on their journey under the Earth - they said their
journey had been a thousand years... (because)
depending on the errors each man had committed
and the number of people he had harmed, he
suffered, successively, ten times for each one. Every
hundred years they paid, because a hundred years

counts as the life of a man, and so it was that evil
works were paid for ten times over. - Plato, *The Republic*

The Cellular Region

The return of the human Essence begins with conception. The trio that starts our life—conception, gestation, birth—is marvellous. It is amazing to think that man begins as a cell, subject to the rapid time of cells, and living in the world of cells. It is extraordinary to know that after about 80 years his human life ends, overcharged with memories. The inner processes that begin conception are extremely rapid, but as time passes become slower. All organic processes become slower.

In fact, the relativity of time does exist. Human gestation lasts 10 lunar months, infancy 100 lunar months, and life more or less 1,000 lunar months.

The electromagnetic trace that the life of a man leaves in the instant of death is imprinted firmly on the conception of the foetus. The path of life is formed with the hoof marks of the "horse of death." Death, judgment, and conception make a perfect trio. A book called *Tibetan Yoga and Secret Doctrines* says:

> *At the moment of death, the four sounds called*
> *"sounds that inspire sacred terror" are heard: that of*
> *the vital force of the element earth, a sound like the*
> *collapse of a mountain; that of the vital force of the*
> *element water, a noise like that of ocean waves; that*
> *of the vital force of the element fire, a sound like that*
> *of a jungle fire; that of the vital force of the element*
> *air, a sound like that of a thousand thunderclaps*
> *echoing simultaneously. The place in which one seeks*
> *shelter, fleeing from these noises is the womb.*

When the zoosperm unites with the ovum, gestation begins. The cell with which human life begins has 48 chromosomes. This clearly speaks of 48 laws that govern the human organism. There are 48 controls that regulate the human organism. The chromosomes are divided into genes. A hundred or so make a chromosome. The total constitution of the human organism is determined by the genes.

Genes are very difficult to study because they are made up of a few molecules. They vibrate rapidly and constitute an intermediary zone between the Molecular World and the Cellular World. The genes move and combine under the radio-active waves emitted by a dying person in his last moments. So the new physical body is the exact result of our past return, the faithful instrument of our Karma.

The life of every human being in the physical world is a repetition of the past life, plus its good and bad consequences. Time is circular, and events are repeated at the correct time and day. This is the law of Recurrence. Everything happens again as it happened before, but with its consequences, good as well as bad. This is the law of Karma, the law of action and consequence.

In fact, the object of the automatic repetition of events is to make us aware of our own errors; that is the law. Unfortunately we can do nothing. Everything is repeated at the correct time, just as the hands of the clock go round.

To change external circumstances, we have to change internally by forming Soul and Spirit, that is to say processing Being. Only the Being can create. Only the Being can change all things. Whoever wants to possess Being has to transmute his sexual, emotional, mental, passionate, motor, sentimental, etc. energies. We have to transmute the base metals, that is to say, our defects, into the purest Gold of the Spirit. Only in this way will we possess Soul and Spirit. The pluralized ego has to die. It is urgent that the Being be born within us.

Life in the cellular world is a tremendous repetition of events, and we can only liberate ourselves from this tragic wheel of fate by dissolving the ego on the basis of supreme Understanding and sanctity, and by forming Soul and Spirit. It is a horrible vicious circle, the Wheel of Samsara.

The Molecular Region

The legend of Zoroaster says:

All those whose good works outweigh their sins, go to Heaven; those whose sins are greater go to Hell; he who has the two equal remains in Hamistikan until the future body or resurrection.

The Molecular Region is the region of Paradise. Those beings who suffered greatly in life and who were relatively good become submerged in the happiness of the Molecular World before taking a new physical body. The molecular regions are saturated in happiness. The human Essences enjoy these ineffable regions in the absence of their pluralized egos. Meanwhile, the egos of the Essences remain in the doorway of mystery, awaiting the new reincarnation. In the absence of the ego, the essences develop happily in Paradise. These beings use the Molecular Body. Those who possess the Christ-Astral shine with glory and are even happier in Paradise. This happiness lies only in the sexual seed, in a germinal state. It germinates and is born when the initiate knows the mysteries of sex. The Christ-Astral is a marvellous body. People who possess this body are truly immortal, since they never lose their consciousness.

As Paradise is molecular, it enters and penetrates all Earth's atmosphere and is especially related to the ionosphere, which is found sixty miles above the Earth's surface. This region is especially pure. Even when the astronauts travel through this area, they can never discover Paradise with their physical senses. We can only see Paradise with the spatial sense. The Gnostic Movement teaches various scientific techniques for opening the spatial sense.

The Molecular Region has various ineffable countries. These are the planes and subplanes that Theosophists and Rosicrucians speak of. In these regions of limitless happiness, the disincarnate live happily until their time runs out. Dawn, day, evening, and night, infancy, adolescence, maturity, and old age govern the whole cosmos, and even the disincarnate are subjected to this law. In time, these fortunate beings have to return to the physical world.

Everything that the disincarnate see is in their minds. The Devachanic states spoken of by the Theosophic and Rosicrucian books affirm this. The state of unconsciousness into which the disincarnated fall under electronic shock is very regrettable because even when they enjoy the happiness of the Molecular Regions they are not sufficiently conscious, as an Adept of the White Lodge would be. Only those who have acquired Soul live conscious of the Superior Regions of the Universe.

The ordinary disincarnated ones project their own desires and aspirations into the molecular atmosphere, and dream of them, living in perfect happiness. Adepts do not dream because they have awakened consciousness and live in this region dedicated to work, in accordance with the great Cosmic Laws, in the laboratory of Nature. This does not mean that the disincarnated do not enjoy the scenery of Paradise. Naturally, they are infinitely happy in their surroundings of happiness.

The Egyptian Book of the Dead, and *The Art of Dying,* from the Middle Ages, teach preparation for death.

Men dedicated solely to material things will not have the good fortune of experiencing the happiness of the Electronic World, due to the state of unconsciousness into which they fall. When these people live in the Molecular World, they spend their holidays dreaming, they drink from the fountain of forgetfulness, and dream delightfully.

The molecular body is a microscope and telescope at the same time. With this body, we can see the infinitely small and the infinitely large. In Paradise, the disincarnated participate in the intimate nature of everything created, penetrating the heart of all that exists. It is better to know things by penetration than by external perception. Life in Paradise would be better if the disincarnated did not project their own desires into the Molecular World. There, each projects images of his own mind into the atmosphere.

The Electronic World

The Electronic World is the Solar World of Light, the world of the Spirit. Those who have Spirit, those who possess an Electronic Body, exercise power over the Molecular, Cellular, and Mineral Worlds. Those who possess an Electronic Body are in a position to help their disciples create their own Souls. Any true instructor teaches his disciples to create Soul. Any man with Soul is a true reformer. A man with Soul can help his disciples, teaching them the theory of acquisition of their Soul. But only a man who has an Electronic Body can work with the embryonic Souls in the same way that a man with a Cellular Body can work with the Earth's minerals.

Certain affirmations saying that human beings have Soul and Spirit have been exaggerated. In fact, within the human Essence there exists a fraction of the Causal Being, but this fraction is only the prime material that life has given us to make Soul.

Whoever makes Soul fuses himself with the great Universal Soul. Whoever makes Spirit is united with the Universal Spirit of Life.

> *Because unto everyone that hath shall be given and*
> *he will have abundance... And throw the useless*
> *servant into the outer darkness. There will be wailing*
> *and the gnashing of teeth.* - Matthew 25:29-30

The fate of the human Essence in the Electronic World after death is fleeting, because the human being is still not prepared for living continuously in this solar region.

There are schools for the creation of Soul, and there are also schools of sexual regeneration for the creation of Spirit. The Gnostic Rosicrucian School is a temple and school at the same time. The Gnostic Movement is closely united to the authentic and legitimate Rosicrucian school, which exists only in the Superior Worlds. Our universal, Christian, Gnostic Movement teaches the real path of regeneration. Our school teaches the creation of Soul and Spirit. Our movement has the most complete esoteric school. Our movement is initiating the new Aquarian Age, in the august thundering of thought.

The Electronic World is marvellous. In the Molecular World, light and sound are diffused one hundred times more rapidly than in the Cellular World, but in the Electronic World they travel instantaneously, not along a line like in the Cellular Region, nor across an area like smell, but across a volume of space, and, being independent of atmosphere, they can travel to the Sun in seven minutes.

In the Electronic World, we are light, and we live in all things. There, we experience the tremendous reality of the unity of life. Electronic bodies move freely with the great light in divine space. The human consciousness, dressed with an electronic body, includes within itself the life and consciousness of all the beings of the Universe. This is Yoga, the union with God.

All those who acquire Spirit have to live the drama of the inner Christ, in their practical lives, their homes, in their towns, among their people. This is a cosmic drama that has existed since before the coming of Jesus. The essence of the drama, its principal event, is the death of the initiate and his supreme surrender to the Father. This occurrence takes place amidst lightning, thunder, and great earthquakes.

The transfiguration of the principal person to the Electronic World, the acquisition of Spirit, is something magnificent and terribly divine. In these instants, the electronic force is displaced, and the vertical fracture of all planes of cosmic consciousness opens the inner worlds to the ordinary perception of the man in the street for a moment. Then, all the marvellous things that the Gospels tell of when Jesus died on the cross take place. The earth trembles, graves open, the saints are resuscitated, and they all cry out, "Truly, this is the Son of God."

A Talk on the Mysteries
of Life and Death

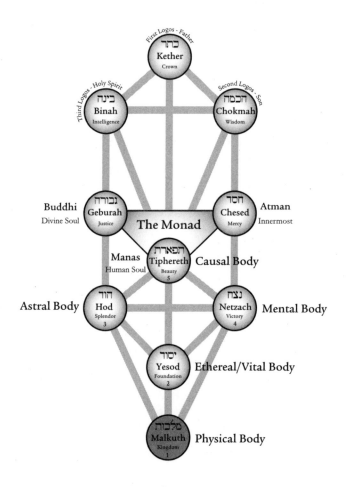

First Logos - Father
כתר
Kether
Crown

Third Logos - Holy Spirit
בינה
Binah
Intelligence

Second Logos - Son
חכמה
Chokmah
Wisdom

Buddhi
Divine Soul
גבורה
Geburah
Justice

The Monad

חסד
Chesed
Mercy
Atman
Innermost

Manas
Human Soul
תפארת
Tiphereth
Beauty
5
Causal Body

Astral Body
הוד
Hod
Splendor
3

נצח
Netzach
Victory
4
Mental Body

יסוד
Yesod
Foundation
2
Ethereal/Vital Body

מלכות
Malkuth
Kingdom
1
Physical Body

A Talk on the Mysteries of Life and Death

We will begin our lecture, and I hope everybody will pay the maximum of attention.

Tonight, I am going to speak about the mysteries of life and death. That is the clear intention of this lecture. We will make a clear differentiation between the Law of the Eternal Return of everything, the Law of Transmigration of Souls, and the Law of Reincarnation.

The time has come to analyze all of this, in order for Gnostic students to be well informed.

It is obvious that the first thing that we need to know in life is, what is the reason of our existence? Why we do exist? What for?

Obviously, if we want to know something about our destiny and about life itself, it is indispensable to know what we are. This is urgent and undeferable.

The Physical and Vital Bodies

The physical body by itself is not all there is to us. A body is made up of organs, and each organ is made up of cells; each cell is composed of molecules, and each molecule of atoms. If we divide any atom, it will liberate energy. Atoms are composed of quarks that revolve around the electrons, protons, neutrons, etc., etc., etc. All of this is known within nuclear physics.

The physical body is composed of different types and sub-types of energy; even human thought is composed of energy. The brain radiates specific type of waves that can be detected. We already know that scientists can measure brain waves with sophisticated instruments (called an electroencephalograph) and that thoughts can be measured as microvolts. So, our organism is composed of different types and subtypes of energies.

Matter is just crystallized energy; that is why Albert Einstein said: "The relative mass of a body exceeds it's net mass by an amount that equals it's kinetic energy, divided by C squared." He also emphatically affirmed that "the energy equivalent of a mass is equal to the mass times the speed of light squared." Therefore, matter is just crystallized energy.

The physical body has a vital organic base. I wish to point emphatically to the Linga-Sarira of Theosophy, the bio-thermal electro-magnetic condensation. Each atom of the Vital Body penetrates each atom of the physical body making it vibrate and spark. In reality, the Vital Double or Vital Body is a type of organic double.

If for example, the arm of that Vital Double comes out of the physical arm, we feel that our hand falls asleep. When that vital arm penetrates once again into the physical arm, when each atom of the Vital Body penetrates into the physical one, it produces a vibration, the vibration that one feels when the arm falls asleep and one has to awaken this arm, feeling a kind of crawling sensation.

If the Vital Body was removed from a person and this Vital Body was not put back within the physical body again, the person would die. So, the Vital Body is interesting. However, that body is just the superior section of the physical body. It is the tetra-dimensional part of the physical body. The Vedic opinion is that the Vital and physical bodies are just one, a unity.

The Ego

If we further study the physical body with its vital organic base we will find that we have the ego. The ego is a conjunction of different inhuman elements that we have within ourselves. It is obvious that those elements are anger, greed, lust, envy, pride, laziness, gluttony, etc., etc., etc. There are so many defects that even having one thousand tongues and a palate of steel, we could not enumerate all of them correctly. So, the ego is just this.

Some people enthrone the ego in their hearts, making an altar and worshipping it. These people are learned ignoramuses that believe that the ego by itself is something divine; really they are perfectly mistaken. Some others divide the "I" into two parts: "superior I" and "inferior I," and they want to have the "inferior I" controlled by the "superior" one. People do not want to understand that the "inferior section" and "superior section" are just two parts of the same thing.

The "I" is time, the "I" by itself is a book with many volumes, in this "I" we find all our aberrations, all our defects, all of what makes us authentic intellectual animals in the most perfect sense of the word. Some believe that we have a divine "alter ego" and worship it, this is really just another way of finding excuses to save the "I," to divinise it. But the "I" is still just the "I," and that's all.

Death

Death itself is a mathematical operation and when this operation ends the only thing that remains are the values. There are positive and negative values, there are good and bad values. Eventually eternity will gobble them up and devour them. In the Astral Light the values attract and reject each other in accordance with the Laws of Universal Emanation. These values are just the inhuman elements that form the ego. These inhuman elements sometimes crash into themselves or just attract or reject themselves.

Death itself is the return to the original starting point. A person is what his or her life is. If one does not work on his own life, if he does not modify it, obviously he is wasting his time because a person is not more than what his life is. We have to work on our own life and to make of it a masterpiece.

Life is like a movie and when the movie ends, we will bring it to eternity. In eternity we relive the life that has just ended. During the first days of this, the deceased person can see the house where he died and even lives in it. If he dies, for example, at the age of eighty years, he will be able to see his grandchildren, to take a seat at the table, etc.; this is to say, the ego will be perfectly convinced that it is still alive and there is nothing in his life that could motivate him to change his mind.

Unfortunately, to the ego nothing changes. He sees life as he always has, seated, for example, in front of the living room table, he will ask for his usual food. Obviously, his relatives will not see him, but their subconsciousness will answer, that subconsciousness will put the food on the table. It's obvious that it will not be physical food because that would be impossible, but it will be mental forms very similar to the food that the deceased person used to eat.

The disembodied can see a wake and he would never think the wake is related to him. He will think the wake belongs to somebody else that has died, but he would never believe that it belongs to him. He feels so alive that he does not even remotely suspect he's dead. If he goes out to the street, he will see the streets in the same way that he saw them when he was alive. Nothing can make him think that something has happened.

If he goes to a church, he will see the priest performing the ritual of the Mass, he will be part of it and will later leave perfectly convinced that he is alive. Nothing can convince him that he is dead. What's more, if somebody were to affirm to him that he is dead, he would smile sceptically and he would not accept that affirmation.

Retrospection After Death

The deceased person has to relive in the Astral World all of his past existences, but he relives it in so natural a form through time, that he becomes identified with it, really enjoying each one of the ages of his already ended life. If he was eighty years old for example, for a while he will be enjoying his grandchildren, taking a seat at the dinner table, using the same bed, etc., but after the passing of time, he will adapt to other circumstances of his own existence.

Soon he will live out the age of seventy years, or the age of seventy-seven, or his sixties, etc.. If he lived in a different house at the age of sixty, he will live in that same house again. He will repeat the same words that he used to and even his psychological field will take the aspect of when he was sixty years old. If at the age of fifty he used to live in another city, he will see himself living in his other house in this other city and so on. During this time his psychological aspects and his physiognomy will transform in accordance with the age that he has to live through.

At the age of twenty years, for example, he will have exactly the same aspects that he had when he was twenty years old. At the age of ten he will see himself as a child, and when the moment comes, he will have ended the review of his past existences. His life will be reduced to mathematic additions and subtractions. All of this is very useful for the consciousness.

In this condition the deceased person will have to present himself to the Courts of Objective Justice or Celestial Justice. These Courts are completely different from the subjective or terrestrial justice. In the Courts of Objective Justice there exists only truth, the law and mercy. It is obvious that beside justice there is always mercy.

There are three paths possible for the deceased person:

1. Vacations in the Superior Worlds (this path is for those that really deserve it).

2. To return in immediate or mediate form to a new womb.

3. To descend into the Infernal Worlds. To fulfill the second death that is mentioned in the Apocalypse of Saint John and in the Gospel of Christ.

Obviously, those that get to ascend to the superior worlds have a season of great happiness.

The Paths of the Dead - Vacation in the Superior Worlds

Normally the Soul, or consciousness, is trapped within the "I" of experiential psychology, within the ego, that, as I said to you, is formed by different inhuman elements.

It happens that those who ascend to the superior worlds leave the ego temporarily. In these cases the Soul, or consciousness, or Essence, gets out of that horrible dungeon of the ego, the "I," to ascend to the famous Devachan that is mentioned by the Hindus, a region of ineffable happiness in the World of the Universal Superior Mind.

In this region they enjoy authentic happiness. There they find their relatives, those that had died before. They meet what we would call their relatives' souls. Later, the consciousness, the Essence, or Soul, also leaves the World of the Mind in order to penetrate into the World of Natural Causes.

The Causal World is grandiose, marvellous. In the Causal World sound all the harmonies of the universe. In this region one really feels the melodies of the infinite. It happens that each planet has multiple sounds, and all of them added together synthesize into a note, this is the keynote of the planet. The conjunction of the keynotes of each world sound marvellously in the huge chorus of starry space and this produces an ineffable joy within the consciousness of all of those beings that enjoy the happiness of the Causal World.

In the Causal World we also find the Lords of the Law who punish and reward men and countries. Here we find the real Men, the Causal Men. We find them working for humanity. In the World of Natural Causes we find the Principalities, the Princes of the Elements, the Princes of Fire, of Air, of the Waters, and Earth.

Life palpitates with intensity in the World of Natural Causes. The Causal World is precious. A profound blue, intense as a star-filled night illuminated by the Moon, shines constantly in the World of Natural Causes. I do not want to say with this that there are not other colors, there are others, but the basic fundamental color is an intense blue, profound as a bright and starry night.

Those that live in that region are happy in the most transcendental sense of the word; however, any reward sooner or later ends. Any reward has a limit and the moment comes, of course, when the Soul that has been in the Causal World has to return, to come back and to descend, inevitably, in order to penetrate into the "I" of experiential psychology. Later, these types of Souls are connected to the fertilized ovum and return into a new physical body, so they come back to the world.

The Paths of the Dead - The Infernal Worlds

The other path is for those that descend to the Infernal Worlds. Those are people that have already fulfilled their time, their cycle of manifestation, or that were very perverse. Undoubtedly, these people devolve among the entrails of the Earth.

In his *Divine Comedy,* Dante Alighieri talks about the nine Dantesque circles and he sees those nine circles inside of the Earth. Our ancestors of Anahuac, in the great Tenochtitlan, speak clearly about the Mictlan (the infernal region that they also locate inside of our terrestrial globe).

To our ancestors of Anahuac, as we have seen in their codex, to pass through the Mictlan was obligatory. They saw it just as a world of probation, where the Souls are tested, and once they have passed through the nine circles, they will be able to penetrate into Eden, that is to say, the terrestrial Heaven.

To the Mohammedan Sufis, the inferno is not a place of punishment, but of instruction and purification for the consciousness.

To Christianity, the inferno is a place of eternal sadness and punishment, however, to the secret circle of Christianity, the hidden part of the Christian religion, it is different. In the hidden part of any Christian movement, in the inner or secret part, is Gnosis. Universal Gnosticism sees the inferno not as a place of eternal and never ending sadness, but as a place of expiation, purification, and education for the consciousness.

Obviously, there exists pain in the Infernal Worlds, because inside of the living Earth, it is terribly dense, especially in the ninth circle, at the core of the terribly hard matter; there the sufferings are unspeakable. Anyway, those that penetrate into the submerged involution of the Mineral Kingdom sooner or later have to pass through what the Christic Gospels call the Second Death.

In studying the Dantesque Infernos, Universal Gnosticism has never believed that punishment should not have a limit. We think that God, being eternally just, would not demand from anyone something more than what he already owes, because any fault, even if it is really grave, has its price. Once that price is paid, we think it would be absurd to keep paying.

Even here, in our subjective terrestrial justice, we can see that if a person goes to jail for a determined transgression, once he has paid it he is free. Not even the terrestrial authorities would accept that a convict should remain in jail after he has paid his time. However, there have been cases when the convicted, once the day of liberty came, did not want to get out; then he had to be taken out by force.

So, every fault has a price. If the terrestrial judges know this, how much more would the divine justice know? Even the gravest faults have their price, but once the price is paid, we have the ticket to freedom.

If things were not like this, God would be a great tyrant and we know very well that beside divine justice there is always mercy. To call God a tyrant in any form would be similar to blasphemy, and frankly we do not like blasphemy.

So, the Second Death is the limit of the punishment in the Dantesque Infernos. Whether the Infernos are called Tartarus in Greece or Averno in Rome, Avitchi in India, or Mictlan in the ancient Tenochtitlan, it doesn't really matter. Every country, every religion, every era or culture, knew of the existence of the Infernos and baptized it with a name.

For the ancient inhabitants of the great Hesperides, the Infernos are the dwelling of Pluto, as we can verify when reading the divine *Aeneid* of Virgil, the Poet of Mantua. So, the Infernos are the cavernous regions in which Aeneas the Trojan found Dido, the queen who killed for love, after she had sworn fidelity to the ashes of Siqueo.

The Second Death is really painful. The ego feels as if it has been divided into different parts, the fingers fall off, its arms, its legs. It suffers through a tremendous breakdown. Moments later, the Essence, the Soul that was trapped inside of the ego, takes the form of an infantile figure; then it becomes a gnome in order to penetrate into the evolution of the mineral elementals.

There are different classes of elementals in Nature. The authorities in this field are Franz Hartmann (he has an interesting book called *The Elementals*), and Paracelsus, the great doctor Philippus Theophrastrus Bombast of Hohenheim (Aureolus Paracelsus).

The elementals are the consciousness of the elements. We know very well that the elements (fire, air, water, earth) are not something physical only, as many learned ignoramuses believe, but the vehicles of simple consciousness. Primigenials, in the most transcendental sense of the word. So the elementals are the conscious principles of the elements.

The Wheel of Life

Now, let's keep going in our explanation. It is obvious that those who have passed through the Second Death will have

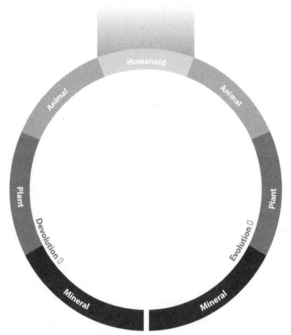

THE WHEEL OF EVOLUTION AND DEVOLUTION

to go to the surface of the world, in order to re-initiate new evolutive processes that obviously will have to begin from the mineral, the stone, and passing to the vegetable, will continue into the animal until finally they will have access to human life. They will then reconquer the human or humanoid state that they had lost.

It is really interesting to see these gnomes among the rocks, they look like small dwarfs, with their big books and long white beards. Obviously, to say this in the 20th century sounds very strange because people have become so complicated. The mind is so deviated from the simple truths of nature that it is hard for our mind to accept these things. I would say, this is a type of knowledge that is accepted by simple, natural people, those that do not have a complicated intellect.

I want to tell you that the mineral elementals, when transitioning and evolving into a plant are really interesting and that each plant is the physical body of a vegetal elemental. The elementals of plants have consciousness, they are very intelligent and there are great esotericists that know how to use or manage them voluntarily. They are really beautiful, and those that know them can control the elements of nature with their help.

Further ahead of the plant elementals, we have the elementals of the animal kingdom. Obviously, only the advanced plant elementals have the right to enter into animal organisms. Evolution in this kingdom always begins in simple organisms, but accordingly they evolve. Life also begins to become more complicated to the point that the animal elemental can take on more complex organic bodies. Later, they can reconquer the human state that they lost in the past.

In the human state, the elemental, the Essence, the consciousness, the Soul (whatever you want to call it or however you like it explained) once again receives 108 existences for the realization of the Inner Self. If the Inner Self realization of the Being is not achieved during the 108 existences then the Wheel of Life continues moving and the Essence has to descend again. The Essence will descend to be among the entrails of the mineral kingdom, in order to eliminate the undesirable elements that in one form or another adhere to the psyche.

In conclusion, the wheel revolves 3,000 times. If within the 3,000 cycles (each one having 108 human existences) the Essence does not attain realization, every door is then closed and the Essence, transformed into an innocent elemental, submerges itself back into the core of the Great Reality, or saying it another way, into the Great Alaya of the Universe, into the Universal Spirit of Life or Parabrahman, as it is called by the Hindus.

So, that is the life for those that descend into the entrails of the Earth after death. We can see that after death some ascend to the superior worlds to experience some vacations, while others descend into the entrails of the Earth and there are still others that return in mediate or immediate form to repeat their existence in this world. They have to return or comeback, to repeat the same life.

Death itself is the return to the original starting point, and I explained that after death, in Eternity, in the Astral Light, we have to relive the existence that we just finished. Now I will tell you, that when we return, we will have to repeat once again in the new life all of our past existence.

QUESTION: Venerable master, you have spoken about the descent of Souls or Essences to the inside of the Earth and their later evolution through the mineral, vegetable and animal kingdoms. You have also said that those Essences have to return after death. Were you speaking about the Doctrine of the Transmigration of the Soul?

SAMAEL AUN WEOR: Well, in the first case, I was speaking about the Law of the Souls' Transmigration and about those Souls that had fulfilled the cycle of 108 existences and the necessity to descend into the entrails of the world. I also said that once the ego was dead, they would be able to come back to a new evolution that goes from the mineral to the man. This is the Doctrine of the Transmigration of the Soul.

Now I am beginning to talk about the Doctrine of Eternal Return of everything and also about the law called the Doctrine of Recurrence.

Return and Recurrence

If, instead of descending to the entrails of the world, one returns in mediate or immediate form to the world, it is obvious that one will have to repeat the same life, the life that has just ended.

You might say such a situation would be very boring. We are all here repeating what we did in our past existence, in our past life. Of course it is really boring! But we are the ones to blame because, as I've said, a man is what his life is; if we do not change our life, we will have to repeat it continuously.

We die and once again we get another physical body. What for? In order to repeat the same life. However, the day comes when we will have to go with our song to another place, when we will have to descend into the entrails of the world, to the Second Death. But these repetitions are not avoidable. These repetitions are known as Law of Recurrence. Everything happens as it happened before. But why, you say? Why does one have to repeat the same mistakes? Well, this has to be explained.

I want you to know that the "I" is not something autonomous or auto-conscious, or individual. Certainly the "I" is an addition of many "I's." Common psychology, modern psychology, believes the "I" is a unity. We see the "I" as an addition of many "I's," because we have one "I" of anger, we have another "I" of greed, another "I" of lust, another "I" of envy, another "I" of laziness, another "I" of gluttony. There are different "I's. There is not one "I," but many "I's" within our organism.

It is obvious that the pluralized "I" is the basis for the Doctrine of the Many "I"s that is taught in oriental Tibet. The great Kabir Jesus confirmed this Doctrine of the Many "I"s. It is said that he removed seven demons from Mary Magdalene's body. There is no doubt that they were the seven capital sins: anger, greed, lust, envy, pride, laziness, gluttony. Each one of them is the head of a legion, and as I have said many times, even if we had a thousand tongues to speak and palate of steel, we would be unable to enumerate all of our defects. Each defect is an "I."

So, we have many I's, defects. If we call them demons, we are not mistaken. In the Christic gospel, a possessed man is asked for his real name and he answers "I am legion, my real name is legion." Each one of us, in reality, is a legion and each I-demon of this legion wants to control the brain, wants to control the principal five centers of the organic machine, wants to be prominent, to go up, to ascend to the top of the ladder.

Each I-demon is like a person inside of our body. If we were to say that within our personality there live many people, we would not be deluded; it is the truth.

So the mechanical repetition of the different events of our past existences is based in the multiplicity of the "I." We will explain this with facts: Suppose that in a past existence, at the age of 30, we had a fight with someone in a bar (something common in life). Obviously the I-defect of anger was the principal persona of this event. After death, that defect remains in Eternity and in our new existence it will be in the bottom of our subconscious, awaiting the age of thirty in order to return to a bar. Within that defect there is resentment and it will wish to meet the person involved in that previous event. At the same time, the other person, the one that was involved in that tragic event, also has his own "I" that wants revenge and that is alive in the bottom of his subconscious, awaiting the moment to enter into activity.

When the age of thirty years comes, the "I" of the person, the I-anger, the "I" that took part in that past tragic event, says within the subconsciousness: "I have to meet that man." On the other hand, the other guy's subconscious says: "I have to find that guy," and telepathically both "I's" decide to meet in some bar. So they will meet physically in the next existence and repeat the event as it happened in the past existence.

All of this escapes our intellect because it is beyond our reasoning. We have been brought to a tragedy, we have been unconsciously taken to repeat the same thing over again.

Now, let us look at another example where someone at the age of thirty had a love affair in his past existence. The "I" of that affair remains alive and after death stays in eternity. When we return into a new organism, that "I" that caused the affair will be alive, waiting in the bottom of the subconscious, in the unconscious levels of the psyche. At the age of thirty, when the age of that affair comes again, the "I" enters again into activity and says: "Well, now is the time, now I will try to find the lady of my dreams." At the same time, the "I" within the lady of his dreams says the same thing, "This is the moment, I will find that gentleman." We don't even notice it, but beyond our reasoning, beyond our intellect, beyond our intelligence, a telepathic appointment is made. Each one will move the physical personality and the affair is once again repeated. This is really how we are. This may sound incredible, but we don't do anything about it. Everything happens to us, as when it rains, or when it thunders.

If one had a problem with material things, then the "I" of that problem will remain alive after death. In the new existence, this "I" will be hidden in the levels of the mind waiting for the moment in order to become active. So, if that problem occurred in the past life at the age of fifty years, then in this present life at the age of fifty that "I" will say: "This is the moment" and the other person with whom one had that problem will certainly also say: "This is the moment." Thus, they will meet again in order to repeat the same discussion.

Well, this indicates that we do not even have free will. Everything happens to us, I repeat, as when it rains or thunders. There is a small margin of free will, but it is very small. Imagine for a moment, a violin inside its case. There is a very small margin of movement for that violin. In this form is our free will. It is almost non-existent, there is only a small margin of free will, it's almost imperceptible. If we know how to use it, then it's possible for us to transform ourselves radically and to become free from the Law of Recurrence, but it is necessary to use that small margin.

In practical life we have to become a little bit more self-aware. When one accepts that one has a psychology, then one begins to observe oneself and when one begins to observe oneself, then one begins to become different.

It is in the street, at home, and at our job where the defects that are hidden appear spontaneously, and if we are as alert and vigilant as the watchman in times of war then we can see them. A discovered defect has to be judged through conscious analysis, reflection and inner meditation—by means of the Being—with the intention to understand the defect. When one comprehends a determined defect, then one is already prepared to disintegrate it atomically.

Is it possible to disintegrate the defect? Yes it is possible, but we need a power that is superior to the mind, because the

DURGA, THE DIVINE MOTHER KUNDALINI, DEFEATS THE DEMON (EGO-DESIRE).

mind by itself cannot fundamentally alter any psychological defect. The mind can classify it with different names, can pass it from one level of understanding to another, can hide it from itself or from other people, it can justify it or condemn it, but it can never alter it radically. We need a power that is superior to the mind, a power that can disintegrate any I-defect. That power is latent in the bottom of our psyche, it is necessary to know that power and to learn to utilize it.

Devi Kundalini & the Disintegration of Defects

In the Orient, in India, that power is called Devi Kundalini, the igneous serpent of our magical powers. In the great Tenochtitlan it was called Tonantzin. In the Middle Ages Alchemists gave it the name Stella Maris, the Virgin of the Sea. Amongst the Hebrews it was called Adonia. Amongst the Cretans it was known by the name of Cibeles. Amongst the Egyptians it was Isis, "the one whose veil no mortal has lifted." Amongst the Christians it is Mary, or Maya, that is to say, God the Mother.

We have thought of God as the Father for a long time, but it is also worthwhile to think of God as the Mother, as Love, as Mercy. God the Mother lives at the bottom of our psyche, that is to say, she is in the Being. I would say to you that God the Mother is a part of our own Being, but derived.

Let us distinguish between the Being and the "I." The Being and the "I" are incompatible, they are like water and oil. They cannot be mixed. The Being is the Being and the reason for it's existence is *to be*. The Being is what has been and what will always be. It is the life that palpitates within each atom, just as it palpitates within each Sun.

So, God the Mother is a derivation of our own Being. This means that each one of us has his own particular, individual Divine Mother Kundalini, as it is called by the Hindus. I believe that in profound meditation we can find the Divine Mother and beg her to disintegrate the I-defect that we have understood perfectly in meditation.

The Divine Mother will act and disintegrate it, will reduce it to cosmic dust. When a defect is disintegrated, it liberates psychic Essence, because inside of every defect there is a percentage of trapped psychic Essence. When a defect is disintegrated, the spiritual Essence is liberated. If two defects are disintegrated, well, more spiritual Essence will be liberated, and if the totality of the psychological defects that we carry within is disintegrated, then we will liberate the consciousness completely.

The Truth

A liberated consciousness is a consciousness that is awakened. An awakened consciousness is a consciousness that will see, hear, and touch the great mysteries of life and death. It is a consciousness that will be able to experience—through itself and directly—that which we call Reality, that which we call the

Truth, which exists far away from the effects of the body and
the mind.

When the great Kabir Jesus was asked about the truth by
Pilate he remained silent, and when the Shakyamuni Buddha,
Gautama, the Prince Siddhartha, was asked the same question, he turned his back and walked away. The truth is the
unknown from moment to moment, from instant to instant.
That which is called truth comes to us only with the death of
the ego.

The truth is something that has to be experienced; I
repeat, it is like when one puts their finger in a flame and is
burned. A theory about the truth is not the truth. A theory
or an opinion, even a respectable and venerable one, is not the
truth. Any idea that we may have about the truth is not the
truth, even if the idea is very bright. Any thesis that we could
create about truth is not the truth. The truth has to be experienced, I repeat, as when one puts their finger into a flame and
is burned.

The truth is far away from the body, the affections, and
the mind and can only be experienced in the absence of the
psychological "I." When the "I" has not been eliminated, the
experience of reality is impossible. The intellect itself, even if it
has bright ideas or is very bright, is not the truth. As Goethe,
the author of *Faust*, said: "Any theory is grey except the green
tree with golden fruits that symbolizes life."

So, we need to disintegrate the psychological "I" to liberate the Essence; only in that way we will experience the truth.

Jesus the Christ said: "Know the truth and it will make
you free" (we need to experience it directly). When somebody
really eliminates the ego and liberates herself from the Law of
Recurrence, she makes her life a masterpiece, and transforms
herself into a genius, into an illuminate, in the most complete
sense of the word.

When somebody liberates his consciousness, obviously
he knows the Truth. The consciousness has to be liberated
and this is impossible to do if the psychological ego is not
eliminated. Those that worship the "I" are self-worshippers by

nature. The "I" is worshipped by megalomaniacs because they are megalomaniacs. The "I" is worshipped by those who are paranoid, because they are paranoid.

Life on the surface of the Earth would be different if we eliminated the Ego, because then the awakened consciousness of everyone would radiate love and there would be peace on the face of the Earth. Peace itself it is not something that is related to peace agreements, armies, the U.N. or something like that. Peace itself is a substance that emanates from the Being, from the entrails of the Absolute. Real peace and happiness cannot exist on the surface of this planet as long as the psychological factors that produce war are still alive within ourselves. It is clear that as long as discord exists within us, there will be discord in the world.

Society itself is the extension of the individual, what a person is, society is, and what outer society is, so is the world. If an individual transforms himself, if a person eliminates the elements of hatred, egotism, violence, discord, etc., this is to say, if someone achieves the elimination of their ego to liberate their consciousness, what will appear in him is what is called love. If every person that lives on the surface of Earth would eliminate their ego, then the masses would be masses of love. There wouldn't be wars or hatred. Real peace cannot exist in the world while ego exists.

Some affirm that from the year 2001 or 2007 on there will come an era of fraternity, love and peace. But, thinking out loud I ask myself, and even I ask you: From where do you think such an era of fraternity, love and peace among "men of good will" will come? From the ego with its hatreds, rancour, envies, ambitions, lusts, etc.? Do you really think that this could happen? Obviously not!

If we really want peace in the world, it's necessary to destroy what we have that is inhuman; the hatred, the envy, the horrible jealousy, the anger that makes us so abominable, the fornication that makes us like beasts. Whilst those causes are still alive in our psyche, the world will not be different, it will become worse because over time the ego will become more powerful and the world will become more tenebrous. To this measure, if we do not work on ourselves, a day will come when we will no longer exist, because we will destroy one another in a violent form.

If the ego were to continue to grow stronger without a limit, as we are now, a time would come when no one could have security in his life, not even at home. In a world in which violence is fully developed, nobody's existence feels secure. So I strongly believe that the solution to all the problems in the world is the elimination of the "I."

Tomorrow we'll celebrate a very important holiday, and it's clear that we shouldn't let this date pass without speaking about it. I am talking about the Day of the Dead Celebration. Tomorrow is the day, and it seems necessary to explain the mysteries of life and death.

The Path

You know very well, my dear brothers and sisters, that the path is very hard. Jesus the Christ spoke about the secret path when he said,

> Strait is the gate, and narrow is the way, which leadeth unto life, and few there be that find it.

Hermes Trismegistus, that thrice great god, the real incarnation of the god Osiris, gave us the marvellous science of Alchemy.

In the Middle Ages, that hermetic science passed from the Arabic world to the lands of Europe, and then the enthusiasm for the hermetic art began to appear everywhere. The doctrine of Hermes contains—in essence and in potence—the greatest keys and the purest knowledge that allows one to walk the "narrow path" that was mentioned by Jeshua ben Pandira, Jesus the Christ. We well know that the Great Kabir in his past existence, before he fulfilled his mission in the holy land, was Jeshua, son of man.

Obviously, "many are called but few are chosen." Certainly, it is possible to count on the fingers of one hand those that have perseverance to achieve the final goal. Fortunately, we have a body of doctrine and principles which provide a basis that, when studied and experienced, can allow us to walk along the path of the razor's edge.

Those that brought forth the doctrine and the principles, the foundations, were always great Avatars. Avatars are Logoic Crystallizations. It is not possible to conceive of a messenger that comes from the heavens except as an emanation, a crystallization or manifestation of the Logos in our world. So, having this foundation, it is necessary to do the work. Only in this form is it possible to achieve final liberation.

Undoubtedly, my dear brothers and sisters, the human species is under the Law of Eternal Return. We have already repeated many times that each cycle of manifestation, each cycle of existences, has 108 lifetimes. If we do not obtain Self-realization, it is obvious that then we will fall under the law that was explained by the great Avatar Krishna who lived about 3000 years before Christ (I am talking about the Law of Souls' Transmigration, or the Metempsychosis of Pythagoras).

Those that do not obtain Self-realization during their 108 existences obviously will have to devolve in the submerged mineral kingdom, finally reaching Ninth Sphere. There they become cosmic dust; in other words, they pass through the Second Death that was mentioned with great wisdom by the great Kabir Jesus.

After this Second Death, in other words, the death of the inhuman elements that we have within, the Essence, the Soul or Immortal Principle, escapes, goes back to the surface, to the light of the sun, to re-initiate a new evolution that obviously will begin from the stone, continuing into the vegetable, later into the animal, finally reconquering the human state, or better said, the humanoid state that we had lost. In the human or humanoid state, we receive once again 108 lifetimes. If we achieve Self-realization in this new cycle of existences it will be extraordinary; if we fail, it is obvious that the process will have to be repeated.

So, my dear brothers and sisters, we either achieve Self-realization or we have to remain in the valley of Samsara, on this great fatal wheel that revolves 3,000 times. Obviously, after the last rotation, the opportunities end and those that did not achieve realization of the self and the initiations will have to submerge themselves into the Universal Spirit of Life, but without mastery. They will have happiness but will not have had the initiations. They will have attained happiness, but will not have attained realization. They will be transformed into elementals of the universe, and that is all!

There is no doubt my dear brothers and sisters, that the 3,000 rotations of the wheel are very painful. Those that have studied profoundly the doctrine that is related to the realization of the Inner Self, of the Being, have reached the conclusion that not all human beings are capable of achieving realization. It is also absolutely true that not all the Monads or Divine Sparks that emanated from the entrails of the Universal Spirit of Life are interested in Mastery. When a Divine Spark really yearns to achieve Mastery, it exerts its Soul, its Essence, and fights in order to achieve it.

In this world we see many people, millions of human beings, that do not have any interest in the realization of the Inner Self, of the Being. Someone could object to this saying that these people do not know Gnosis. This is correct to a certain point, however, when we divulged the teaching everywhere, some people came to the call and others were just indifferent, and these unfortunately are the majority.

So, we know when there exists inquietude and yearning. If somebody wants to achieve mastery, he works. When somebody has that yearning, obviously he is moved from his most intimate realities, they are working in secret. But, who is working him? His own Divine Spark, his real Being, because this spark, by itself, wants to achieve Mastery. But I repeat, not all the Virginal Sparks yearn for Mastery.

On this day, the Day of the Dead, it is necessary to reflect. The Great Law does not abandon those that do not yearn for mastery, nor do they leave those that fight in order to achieve it and fail. The Omnimerciful takes cares of all creatures and does not abandon anyone.

Egypt was very advanced in the field of embalming and mummification. There is no doubt that the mummies in Egypt are extraordinary. The Egyptians had the capacity to preserve living bodies, not through hibernation, but through a type of mummification that allowed bodies to exist for million of years.

Even now in the land of the Pharaohs, underground and under the pyramids or in secret places, there are living bodies of Masters (mummies) that date from 3,000 to 4,000 and even 10,000 years before Christ. These Masters will once again penetrate into their physical bodies that sleep underground, as is written in the *Book of the Dead*, to initiate in the world a new Neptunian-Amentian era.

Getting to the bottom of this knowledge, the Egyptians, Tibetans, Aztecs, and Mayans taught that it is possible to achieve liberation after death and not come back to this hard world again. Those that proceed in this way obviously do so, but without realization of the self.

Because there are few that achieve realization of the self, it is always preferable to get emancipated from the painful valley of Samsara. It is not mandatory and it is not indispensable to wait until the 3,000th rotation of the Wheel of Samsara. Those that yearn for liberation can achieve it even if they do not obtain Mastery, because not all human beings are born to attain Mastery, or to become Mahatmas, or Logos. There always exists a door of escape for those that feel they are not capable to do the Great Work.

Obviously, if after the 3,000th cycle we have to penetrate into the Universal Spirit of Life without self-realization, meaning again, that we did not work on ourselves, then it is preferable to be liberated at once from this fatal wheel. In this form we would avoid the descent into the Infernal Worlds and the terrible sufferings of the valley of sadness after each cycle of manifestation.

The Two Ways

There are two ways to achieve liberation, two ways to liberate ourselves from this valley of Samsara. The first is to become Self-realized, transformed into a Mahatma or Logos; the other, as simple elementals, without realization of the Inner Self. Everyone has to reflect and to select their path. And once it is selected, we have to be serious, because once we step onto the Secret Path, it is not possible to come back.

That is why, in the Tibetan Mysteries, when somebody is going to receive the initiation, the priests play their trumpets (made of human bones), at the same time they warn the neophyte: "Stop! Do not try to walk on the path that follows after the threshold. Remember that the path of initiation is full of tears, pains and suffering... You can still be happy with the religion that was taught to you, and live in the heavens of nature, in the land of the Devas, of the Holy Gods! Why do you insist on following the Secret Path?"

If the neophyte, after all this says: "Nothing can stop me, I will walk on the path of the razor's edge. I am going to follow the path of realization, nothing can stop me," obviously, he or she will receive the initiation. But if he were to weaken, then he would have to follow the path of common emancipation, liberation without realization of the self. It will not be a Sun, but it will be a star.

The path of emancipation through comprehension does not transform us into gods, it only allows us to escape as elementals and to live in the Universal Spirit of Life forever.

It is not an obligation to continue until the 3,000th cycle of the Wheel of Samsara. Those that do not want to live, those that have become disenchanted with life, those that have drunk from the chalice of all bitterness and do not feel prepared to walk on the path that will transform us into Gods beyond good and evil, can walk on the Path of the Minor Effort, the path that can only transform us into elementals, into small elemental Buddhas, the path that allows us to return to the Great Reality forever.

Obviously, those that do not achieve realization and that have ended their cycle of manifestation, normally have to descend into the entrails of the abyss and suffer terribly in order to pass through the Second Death. After that, comes the emancipation of the Essence. This Essence, transformed into an elemental, will initiate a new evolution. Naturally, what we have to do, or what nature will do with us within the entrails of the earth, can be done by us voluntarily, here and now, so that we could avoid the descent into the entrails of the abyss.

If nature will disintegrate ego, the myself, involuntarily, then we should do it voluntarily and in this way avoid the submerged mineral kingdom. If after the Second Death we will be transformed into elementals, it is better to be transformed into elementals here and now, and avoid passing through that vast bitterness. So there is mercy; for the Eternal Cosmic Common Father, the Omnimerciful, never leaves anyone.

In death there are extraordinary mysteries. Those who really want emancipation, to not come back, forever, have to start by knowing the doctrine. It isn't possible to demand from a human creature the radical elimination of the ego, here and now, if it is not prepared. But it is possible for any creature, if he wants, to eliminate his ego, the "I," even if it is only partially done, for after death, there can be an opportunity to continue the rest of the work.

But here is the problem: if we have a sleeping consciousness, we will have to return anyway. Then what do we have to do in order to avoid returning to this valley of tears? Awaken the consciousness! But when do we have to do this? After death or now? It is clear that we have to work in order to awaken the consciousness! Is there some science that would allow us to achieve awakening? Yes, it exists, and we have taught it, and we will keep teaching it throughout our different lectures.

The one that awakens can select his path; the one that awakens will be able to continue the work after death, and if he does not want to come back, he will not return. So, how can someone who is asleep avoid coming back to this valley of tears? Is it impossible. First, it is necessary to awaken; once awakened, we will be able to continue the work after death.

Tests After Death

However, it is obvious that a deceased person will be tested if she does not want to come back. First of all, after death the person passes through a fainting of three days; after this the person feels better and rejuvenated. If the deceased person is vigilant and alert, if she really does not have her consciousness in an asleep state, and if she really yearns not to return, she will be able to avoid the return to this valley of bitterness. I repeat, if she does not want to return, she will be tested.

The Divine Mother and the Father that are in secret (or the Father-Mother, because everyone has their Father that is in secret and their Divine Mother Kundalini), will test her. They will take on, in front of her, a terrible form, a supra-human figure, with the intention to test the deceased person; but if she remains solid as steel, it is certain that she will succeed. But that is not the only test, there are many others.

The deceased person that does not want to come back should not feel any attraction to his relatives. He should not feel any attraction towards his brothers, sisters, sons, daughters, etc., because he will hurt himself. If he is attracted by those beloved beings that he left in the world, it is clear that he will return, he will come back once again. If the person does not want to come back, it's necessary to not feel attracted to those that we have left in this valley of tears. After death, nature has many systems to make us return, and this is something that we have to understand.

Before everything else, it is important for you to know that after death we have to review the existence that just ended. We will start from the last moment before our agony. We will have the inclination to live in the same house that we lived in before we were dead. We'll want to walk through the same streets that we used to walk on. In other words, we will have to relive all our actions, and we will do so in keeping with the need to review the different ages of the past existence that just ended.

It is clear that this is not a mere intellectual retrospection. After death one has to relive all the events, situations, and occurrences of the past life, and in accordance with this, one assumes the same aspects that one had in each one of his ages. If one was an elder, one will see oneself being that elder. After this, being a middle aged person, being a young adult, later a teenager and finally a child. One will relive all of his existence with the intention of seeing the balance of his good and bad actions.

I want you to know, my dear brothers and sisters, that the Being is composed of different parts. For example, within ourselves exists in the Being (or a part of the Being), a part that we could call the Good Angel. There also exists a part that we could call the Bad Angel, not because it's bad, no. It's because it is the aspect of the Being that's in charge of taking note of our personal errors. The Good Angel takes note of our good actions. The Good and Bad Angels are not strange persons. They are part of our own Individual Spirit, of our own intimate Being.

After death for example, the Good Angel will count with small stones the quantity of good actions that we have done, and we will also see the Bad Angel (it is not that he is evil, it is just that he counts our errors and he is a part of our Being) counting with small black stones our incorrect acts, but this count will be done only after we have relived our previous existence.

All of our past existence is reduced to numbers, to additions of good and bad actions. Obviously, at the end of the retrospection and after the balance, the inventory that our own Being has done will be judged by the Lords of Karma who will determine the existence that we will have next. However, if we do not want to return, we have to have been preparing ourselves during our existence in order to do this. If we are awakened, we will be able to defend ourselves, we will be able to beg our Mother Kundalini for the forgiveness of our errors. We will be able to concentrate on a part of our Being called The Great Merciful, and we will get help, but if our Karma was really bad, and in life we were excessively perverse, then obviously we will have to go through the submerged involution in the Infernal Worlds. There will be no other solution, or at the very least we will have to return once again against our will. But if the Karma is not so bad, if there were more good actions than bad ones, if during life we were really concerned about the elimination of the ego, the myself, if we were charitable, we will have the right to defend ourselves, with cosmic capital on our side.

Closing Wombs

However, it is necessary to not be attracted to human wombs. The human spirit can pass through a mountain and nothing can stop him; the only thing that can stop him is a womb. This is a problem. The wind of Karma will howl, a cold hurricane will approach the deceased person. Multiple visions of terrible beings will try to frighten him, but if he remains firm in the desire to not return, he will be successful. But if he yet feels in danger of falling into a human womb, he will have to learn how to close wombs, and there are many systems in the Inner Worlds. The deceased person suddenly feels that is raining, thundering and flashing, there is lightning and a lot of rain. This is the Law of Karma, trying to connect him to a womb. If he remains serene and immutable, he will be closing wombs.

The untrained one will run trying to find refuge in a cavern, trying to avoid the storm, and when he tries to go back outside, he will feel as if he is tied to that cavern. Yes, he was connected to a womb, to an embryo. That cavern was a womb. So, it is necessary to learn to close wombs, if we do not want to return.

The deceased person will also see many creatures (men and women) copulating. If he is suddenly attracted to a determined house, or feels sympathy for one member of the couple and antipathy for the other, obviously right then and there he will have to return and come back.

A deceased person that feels sympathy for the woman in the couple is certainly attracted and will reborn within that space (or womb) with a masculine body, and vice versa. If he feels sympathy for the man in the couple and antipathy for the female, then obviously he will be born there with a feminine body.

So we are attracted to determined places or homes in accordance with the Law of Karma; and if we are beyond sympathy and antipathy, if during our life we had been practicing avoiding those feelings, we will not penetrate into any human embryo, we will not penetrate into any womb.

Another system to avoid falling into a womb is profound meditation. To learn to achieve the stillness and silence of the mind in order to reach the Illuminating Void within ourselves. If we can remain in the Illuminating Void, we will avoid the attraction of the wombs, we will close wombs.

In life, those that want liberation even in the elemental state, without Self-realization, have to receive instruction about it, have to fight for the elimination of ego, the "I," the myself, to walk through the straight path, to tread the path of sanctification, to awaken the consciousness, to learn to live consciously in the Superior Worlds.

In order to awaken consciousness it is necessary to work, here and now. We have taught the science to awaken consciousness, it is in my books. I know you have read it, but what really counts is to practice it.

Those that can avoid the attraction to the valley of Samsara will be able to be reborn after death, only not with a physical body. They will be reborn in a heaven in some type of superior kingdom. It could be in the Kingdom of Gautama Shakyamuni, or in the Kingdom of Maitreya, or in the Kingdom of the Long Hairs, or in the one of Supreme Happiness; this is a supra-normal birth.

There also exists those that are reborn in the inferno; that is the case of those that have ended their cycle of births and deaths, but those that yearn for liberation can be reborn in supra-normal form, in any of those kingdoms of the Superior Worlds. After having been reborn in any of those kingdoms, we will then devote ourselves intensively to the work of eliminating the inhuman elements that we carry within. The intention will be to clean up the Essence, to make it transparent as crystal without the adherence of terrestrial dust. It is obvious that those that want to do this had to have previously passed through some esoteric training here in the physical world.

Stages of the Minor Path

It is written that what a Master does extensively in order to achieve Mastery, to become a Dhyani-Choan, a Kumara, has to be done in a lesser degree by the one that does not yearn for Self-realization, the one that only wants to avoid the valley of Samsara. It is written that the path is divided into four stages.

The first we could denominate as Disciple or "Chela." The second, as Initiate or a person that is "initiated." The third as Arhat or Perfect Man, and the fourth as Mahatma, or Great Soul. These four stages are represented in many temples and ancient monuments. We can see it in the Pyramid of Sun, in Teotihuacan, etc. What the Master has to do on a great scale has to be done on a small scale for the one that wants to avoid the valley of Samsara, this valley of tears. If the Master has become a great Buddha, a god, then the one that wants to avoid this valley will become an elemental Buddha.

If a solar system exists in the Macrocosmos, then it also exists in a molecule, is this not so ? What is a molecule ? Is it not a solar system in miniature? So, what the Adept does through realization of the self is transform himself in a Cosmocreator, into a Dhyani-Choan, a Son of the Flame, a Kumara. It has to be done by the devout yogi, on a smaller scale, transforming himself into an elemental Buddha and passing through the four stages in an incipient form.

The Essence will progress through four stages:

The first stage we can call Nirmanakaya, even though I do not want to state, based on this statement, that an elemental will be a Nirmanakaya who has renounced Nirvana in a conscious and positive way, or something like that. To the contrary, this elemental will live within a kind of Illuminating Void, like a Nirmanakaya, but this elemental will not unfold as a Nirmanakaya form.

The second stage we can call Sambogakaya (this is an experience of the Illuminating Void, only at a much deeper level, more profound, and accompanied with wisdom). The Essence (elemental) will not enjoy a body of Sambogakaya because it has never created it, but it will pass through an analogous or similar state, in its return to the Great Reality.

The third stage is Addikaya, an illuminated spiritual intelligence. The Essence (elemental) will not have the intelligence of a Logos, neither of Hermes Trismegistus, nor of a Kumara, but of an innocent elemental.

In the fourth stage, the Essence (elemental) will have the reward that Dharmakayas receive. Finally, that pure Essence united with the Monad will submerge itself forever into the Supreme Parabrahma, or in other words, into the Great Ocean of the Universal Spirit of Life. The Essence (elemental) will not be a God, but a spark of the Eternal. It will be liberated from the wheel of birth and death, but it will not be Self-realized. It will be a spark of Divinity without Self-realization, without mastery, but happy, and that is all.

Not everyone is correctly prepared to walk on the straight and narrow path that leads to light, and this is something that we have to reflect on. Those who are not ready, those that in their consciousness feel that they are not capable, can start with the elimination of the ego to awaken the consciousness and seriously begin to tread through the path of sanctity.

The last thought of the dying one is definitive. If that dying person does not want to comeback, if he does not want to return, he can escape and not return, but for this you cannot have really bad Karma. There are people that have such hard Karma because of their perversities, that naturally they will have to come back.

The worst part is that the majority of people will have to descend. Instead of being reborn and returning to this world, they will have to transfer their existences, whether they want to or not, to the Infernal Worlds, and unfortunately this is the case for the majority of people.

My dear brothers and sisters, on this night, on the eve of the Day of the Dead, we have to reflect. We have to put the right hand on the heart and ask ourselves, "'Do I really want to walk on the path of the razor's edge, and work on the realization of the Inner Self, the Being?" Perhaps I am not capable and that is not my yearning. But, if my desire is to leave forever, then I will make a decision to begin the awakening of consciousness. I will make the decision to work with our systems in order to achieve that self-awakening, eliminating the ego through the teaching that we have given in clear and precise form.

So, we are faced with a dilemma. We either follow the path of the razor's edge that will let us achieve the realization of the Inner Self, of the Being, or we do not follow it. If we are not able to follow it, if we feel that we are not capable, then it is better to make a decision towards coming back to this valley of tears forever. We have to make a decision, nobody can do it for us.

QUESTION: Master, you were saying that some Monads are interested in realization of the self and others are not, even though all of them emanate from the Absolute. I thought that all of them had the duty of achieving Self-realization. Could you speak about this?

SAMAEL AUN WEOR: I hear your words and I will answer with pleasure. First of all, my friends, I want you to understand that God, the Universal Spirit of Life, is not dictatorial. If that which is the reality, which is the Truth, which is not of time, was dictatorial, what could be our destiny? Friends, God respects in himself his own freedom. With this I want to say to you that amongst the core of Divinity, there are no dictatorships. Every divine spark, every Monad, has absolute freedom to accept or to reject the path of mastery. Is this clear?

QUESTION: With your explanation, Master, could we say that the Monad is responsible when the Essence goes to the inferno?

SAMAEL AUN WEOR: I see a lady in the auditorium that with sincerity has asked a question, and it is evident that I will enjoy answering.

Ladies and gentlemen, when a Divine Monad wants mastery, it is obvious that to achieve it, it has to work with intensity on its Essence from within, from the most profound recesses. It is clear that if the Monad does not have an interest in attaining mastery, it will never awaken in the Essence any intimate aspiration. Obviously, in this case, the Essence without any yearning, trapped in the ego, will enter into the Infernal Worlds. So my answer is emphatic in saying: the Monad is guilty of the Essence's failure.

If the Monad would really work the Essence, it is obvious that it would never descend to the Tartarus as a failure. In millenarian Tibet, the Bardo Thodol guides the deceased people who want to achieve liberation and not return to the bitterness of the world. In the sacred land of the Pharaohs, many Souls would escape from the cloak of Samsara after having worked on the elimination of the ego. Terrible tests await the deceased people who do not want to return to this world. When they successfully pass these tests, they can penetrate into the suprasensible kingdoms. In those regions, they are instructed and helped in order to happily submerge themselves as innocent children into the Great Ocean. Many of those souls will return in the Golden Age, after the great cataclysm, in order to continue to work on their realization of the Inner Self.

Obviously, it is intelligent to retire on time, before our cycle of existences has ended. It is preferable to retire from the school of life rather than be expelled. The submerged involution amongst the entrails of the earth, in the tenebrous Tartarus, is certainly very painful...

Glossary

Arcanum: (Latin. plural: arcana). A secret, a mystery. The root of the term "ark" as in the Ark of Noah and the Ark of the Covenent.

Astral: This term is dervied from "pertaining to or proceeding from the stars," but in the esoteric knowledge it refers to the emotional aspect of the fifth dimension, which in Hebrew is called Hod.

Astral Body: What is commonly called the Astral Body is not the true Astral Body, it is rather the Lunar Protoplasmatic Body, also known as the Kama Rupa (Sanskrit, "body of desires") or "dream body" (Tibetan rmi-lam-gyi lus). The true Astral Body is Solar (being superior to Lunar Nature) and must be created, as the Master Jesus indicated in the Gospel of John 3:5-6, "Except a man be born of water and of the Spirit, he cannot enter into the kingdom of God. That which is born of the flesh is flesh; and that which is born of the Spirit is spirit." The Solar Astral Body is created as a result of the Third Initiation of Major Mysteries (Serpents of Fire), and is perfected in the Third Serpent of Light. In Tibetan Buddhism, the Solar Astral Body is known as the illusory body (sgyu-lus). This body is related to the emotional center and to the sephirah Hod.

"Really, only those who have worked with the Maithuna (White Tantra) for many years can possess the Astral Body." - Samael Aun Weor, *The Elimination of Satan's Tail*

Centers, Seven: The human being has seven centers of psychological activity. The first five are the Intellectual, Emotional, Motor, Instinctive, and Sexual Centers. However, through inner development one learns how to utilize the Superior Emotional and Superior Intellectual Centers. Most people do not use these two at all.

Chakra: (Sanskrit) Literally, "wheel." The chakras are subtle centers of energetic transformation. There are hundreds of chakras in our hidden physiology, but seven primary ones related to the awakening of consciousness.

"The chakras are points of connection through which the divine energy circulates from one to another vehicle of the human being." - Samael Aun Weor, *Aztec Christic Magic*

Consciousness: "Wherever there is life, there exists the consciousness. Consciousness is inherent to life as humidity is inherent to water." - Samael Aun Weor, *Fundamental Notions of Endocrinology and Criminology*

From various dictionaries: 1. The state of being conscious; knowledge of one's own existence, condition, sensations, mental operations, acts, etc. 2. Immediate knowledge or perception of the presence of any object, state, or sensation. 3. An alert cognitive state in which you are aware of yourself and your situation. In Universal Gnosticism, the range of potential consciousness is allegorized in the Ladder of Jacob, upon which the angels ascend and descend. Thus there are higher and lower levels of consciousness, from the level of demons at the bottom, to highly realized angels in the heights.

"It is vital to understand and develop the conviction that consciousness has the potential to increase to an infinite degree." - The 14th Dalai Lama.

"Light and consciousness are two phenomena of the same thing; to a lesser degree of consciousness, corresponds a lesser degree of light; to a greater degree of consciousness, a greater degree of light." - Samael Aun Weor, *The Esoteric Treatise of Hermetic Astrology*

Devachan: In the lecture "The Mysteries of Life and Death," Samael Aun Weor describes the Devachan as "a region of ineffable happiness in the World of the Universal Superior Mind." And in "Mental Representations," he says, "The dead commonly waste much time in the Devachan. I will not deny that this Devachan is a place of happiness and delights, but the figures that make life in the Devachan agreeable are merely living representations of the families, parents, and friends they left on Earth. In one word, the forms of the Devachan are living mental representations, or effigies. They result in a bizarre nature, that is why I say they waste too much time in the Devachan, but they are happy in this place. They feel accompanied by the loved ones they left on Earth. They do not even remotely notice that this world of happiness is full of mental effigies. If they noticed, they would lose the Devachan for themselves."

Devolution: (Latin) From devolvere: backwards evolution, degeneration. The natural mechanical inclination for all matter and energy in nature to return towards their state of inert uniformity. Related to the Arcanum Ten: Retribution, the Wheel of Samsara. Devolution is the inverse process of evolution. As evolution is the complication of matter or energy, devolution is the slow process of nature to simplify matter or energy by applying forces to it. Through devolution, protoplasmic matter and energy descend, degrade, and increase in density within the infradimensions of nature to finally reach the center of the earth where they attain their ultimate state of inert uniformity. Devolution transfers the psyche, moral values, consciousness, or psychological responsibilities to inferior degradable organisms (Klipoth) through the surrendering of our psychological values to animal behaviors, especially sexual degeneration.

Dhyan-Choan: (Sanskrit) "Lord of the Light." A Cosmocreator or Elohim. The Divine Intelligences supervising the cosmos. "A Dhyan Chohan is one who has already abandoned the four bodies of sin, which are the physical, astral, mental, and causal bodies. A Dhyan Chohan only acts with his Diamond Soul. He has already liberated himself from Maya (illusion); thus, he lives happily in Nirvana." - Samael Aun Weor, *The Revolution of Beelzebub*

Ego: The multiplicity of contradictory psychological elements that we have inside are in their sum the "ego." Each one is also called "an ego" or an "I." Every ego is a psychological defect which produces suffering. The ego is three (related to our Three Brains or three centers of psychological processing), seven (capital sins), and legion (in their infinite variations). "The ego is the root of ignorance and pain." - Samael Aun Weor, *The Esoteric Treatise of Hermetic Astrology* "The Being and the ego are incompatible. The Being and the ego are like water and oil. They can never be mixed... The annihilation of the psychic aggregates (egos) can be made possible only by radically comprehending our errors through meditation and by the evident Self-reflection of the Being." - Samael Aun Weor, *The Pistis Sophia Unveiled*

Evolution: "It is not possible for the true Human Being (the Self-realized Being) to appear through the mechanics of evolution. We know very well that evolution and its twin sister devolution are nothing else but two laws which constitute the mechanical axis of all Nature. One evolves to a certain perfectly defined point, and then the devolving process follows. Every ascent is followed by a descent and vice-versa." - Samael Aun Weor, *Revolutionary Psychology*. "Evolution is a process of complication of energy." - Samael Aun Weor, *The Perfect Matrimony*

Gnosis: (Greek) Knowledge.

1. The word Gnosis refers to the knowledge we acquire through our own experience, as opposed to knowledge that we are told or believe in. Gnosis - by whatever name in history or culture - is conscious, experiential knowledge, not merely intellectual or conceptual knowledge, belief, or theory. This term is synonymous with the Hebrew "daath" and the Sanskrit "jna."

2. The tradition that embodies the core wisdom or knowledge of humanity.

"Gnosis is the flame from which all religions sprouted, because in its depth Gnosis is religion. The word "religion" comes from the Latin word "religare," which implies "to link the Soul to God"; so Gnosis is the very pure flame from where all religions sprout, because Gnosis is Knowledge, Gnosis is Wisdom." - Samael Aun Weor, *The Esoteric Path*

"The secret science of the Sufis and of the Whirling Dervishes is within Gnosis. The secret doctrine of Buddhism and of Taoism is within Gnosis. The sacred magic of the Nordics is within Gnosis. The wisdom of Hermes, Buddha, Confucius, Mohammed and Quetzalcoatl, etc., etc., is within Gnosis. Gnosis is the Doctrine of Christ." - Samael Aun Weor, *The Revolution of Beelzebub*

Hydrogen: (From *hydro-* water, *gen-* generate, genes, genesis, etc.) The hydrogen is the simplest element on the periodic table and in Gnosticism it is recognized as the element that is the building block of all forms of matter. Hydrogen is a packet of solar light. The solar light (the light that comes from the sun) is the reflection of the Okidanok, the Cosmic Christ, which creates and sustains every world. This element is the fecundated water, generated water (hydro). The water is the source of all life. Everything that we eat, breathe and all of the impressions that we receive are in the form of various structures of hydrogen. Samael Aun Weor often will place a note (Do, Re, Mi...) and a number related with the vibration and atomic weight (level of complexity) with a particular hydrogen. For example, Samael Aun Weor constantly refers to the Hydrogen Si-12. "Si" is the highest note in the octave and it is the result of the notes that come before it. This particular hydrogen is always related to the forces of Yesod, which is the synthesis and coagulation of all food, air and impressions that we have previously received. Food begins at Do-768, air begins at Do-384, and impressions begin at Do-48.

Illuminating Void: Emptiness. Satori. Sunyata.

"The Illuminating Void is impossible to describe in human words. It is indefinable or indescribable. As was said by the Zen teacher Huai Jang: "Whatever is said misses the main point." Buddhist teachings about Emptiness are comprehensive and profound and require much study before being understood. Only in the absence of the ego can we directly experience Illuminating Emptiness." - Samael Aun Weor, *The Mystery of the Golden Blossom*

Initiation: The process whereby the Innermost (the Inner Father) receives recognition, empowerment and greater responsibilities in the Internal Worlds, and little by little approaches His goal: complete Self-realization, or in other words, the return into the Absolute. Initiation NEVER applies to the "I" or our terrestrial personality.

"Nine Initiations of Minor Mysteries and seven great Initiations of Major Mysteries exist. The INNERMOST is the one who receives all of these Initiations. The Testament of Wisdom says: "Before the dawning of the false aurora upon the earth, the ones who survived the hurricane and the tempest were praising the INNERMOST, and the heralds of the aurora appeared unto them." The psychological "I" does not receives Initiations. The human personality does not receive anything. Nonetheless, the "I" of some Initiates becomes filled with pride when saying 'I am a Master, I have such Initiations.' Thus, this is how the "I" believes itself to be an Initiate and keeps reincarnating in order to "perfect itself", but, the "I" never ever perfects itself. The "I" only reincarnates in order to satisfy desires. That is all." - Samael Aun Weor, *The Aquarian Message*

Internal Worlds: The many dimensions beyond the physical world. These dimensions are both subjective and objective. To know the objective internal worlds (the Astral Plane, or Nirvana, or the Klipoth) one must first know one's own personal, subjective internal worlds, because the two are intimately associated.

"Whosoever truly wants to know the internal worlds of the planet Earth or of the solar system or of the galaxy in which we live, must previously know his intimate world, his individual, internal life, his own internal worlds. Man, know thyself, and thou wilt know the Universe and its Gods. The more we explore this internal world called "myself," the more we will comprehend that we simultaneously live in two worlds, in two realities, in two confines: the external and the internal. In the same way that it is indispensable for one to learn how to walk in the external world so as not to fall down into a precipice, or not get lost in the streets of the city, or to select one's friends, or not associate with the perverse ones, or not eat poison, etc.; likewise, through the psychological work upon oneself we learn how to walk in the internal world, which is explorable only through Self-observation." - Samael Aun Weor, *Revolutionary Psychology*

Through the work in Self-observation, we develop the capacity to awaken where previously we were asleep: including in the objective internal worlds.

Karma: (Sanskrit, literally "deed"; derived from kri, "to do...") The Law of Cause and Effect.

"Be not deceived; God is not mocked: for whatsoever a man soweth, that shall he also reap." - Galatians 6:7

Kaya: (Sanskrit) Mahayana Buddhism describes perfect Buddhahood in terms of kayas or bodies. There are varying ways of understanding the kayas.

1. Dharmakaya: Truth-body, or Formless body, related to the Absolute and visible only to inhabitants of its realm.

2. Rupakaya (body of Form) which is divided into two more:

a. Sambogokaya (Body of Perfect Enjoyment), the "spontaneous clarity" aspect of the buddha, which is perceptible only to highly-realized beings.

b. Nirmanakaya (Body of Manifestation), the compassionate aspect of the buddha, which appears in the world.

Kundalini: "Kundalini, the serpent power or mystic fire, is the primordial energy or Sakti that lies dormant or sleeping in the Muladhara Chakra, the centre of the body. It is called the serpentine or annular power on account of serpentine form. It is an electric fiery occult power, the great pristine force which underlies all organic and inorganic matter. Kundalini is the cosmic power in individual bodies. It is not a material force like electricity, magnetism, centripetal or centrifugal force. It is a spiritual potential Sakti or cosmic power. In reality it has no form. [...] O Divine Mother Kundalini, the Divine Cosmic Energy that is hidden in men! Thou art Kali, Durga, Adisakti, Rajarajeswari, Tripurasundari, Maha-Lak-shmi, Maha-Sarasvati! Thou hast put on all these names and forms. Thou hast manifested as Prana, electricity, force, magnetism, cohesion, gravitation in this universe. This whole universe rests in Thy bosom. Crores of salutations unto thee. O Mother of this world! Lead me on to open the Sushumna Nadi and take Thee along the Chakras to Sahasrara Chakra and to merge myself in Thee and Thy consort, Lord Siva. Kundalini Yoga is that Yoga which treats of Kundalini Sakti, the six centres of spiritual energy (Shat Chakras), the arousing of the sleeping Kundalini Sakti and its union with Lord Siva in Sahasrara Chakra, at the crown of the head. This is an exact science. This is also known as Laya Yoga. The six centres are pierced (Chakra Bheda) by the passing of Kundalini Sakti to the top of the head. 'Kundala' means 'coiled'. Her form is like a coiled serpent. Hence the name Kundalini." - Swami Sivananda, *Kundalini Yoga*

Logos: (Greek) means Verb or Word. In Greek and Hebrew metaphysics, the unifying principle of the world. The Logos is the manifested deity of every nation and people; the outward expression or the effect of the cause which is ever concealed. (Speech is the "logos" of thought). The Logos has three aspects, known universally as the Trinity or Trimurti. The First Logos is the Father, Brahma. The Second Logos is the Son, Vishnu. The Third Logos is the Holy Spirit, Shiva. One who incarnates the Logos becomes a Logos.

"The Logos is not an individual. The Logos is an army of ineffable beings." - Samael Aun Weor, *Endocrinology & Criminology*

Magic: The word magic is derived from the ancient word "mag" that means priest. Real magic is the work of a priest. A real magician is a priest.

"Magic, according to Novalis, is the art of influencing the inner world consciously." - Samael Aun Weor, *The Mystery of the Golden Blossom*

"When magic is explained as it really is, it seems to make no sense to fanatical people. They prefer to follow their world of illusions." - Samael Aun Weor, *The Revolution of Beelzebub*

Mantra: (Sanskrit, literally "mind protection") A sacred word or sound. The use of sacred words and sounds is universal throughout all religions and mystical traditions, because the root of all creation is in the Great Breath or the Word, the Logos. "In the beginning was the Word..."

Master: Like many terms related to spirituality, this one is grossly misunderstood. Samael Aun Weor wrote while describing the Germanic Edda, "In this Genesis of creation we discover Sexual Alchemy. The Fire fecundated the cold waters of chaos. The masculine principle Alfadur fecundated the feminine principle Nifflheim, dominated by Surtur (the Darkness), to bring forth life. That is how Ymir is born, the father of the giants, the Internal God of every human being, the Master." Therefore, the Master is the Innermost, Atman, the Father.

"The only one who is truly great is the Spirit, the Innermost. We, the intellectual animals, are leaves that the wind tosses about... No student of occultism is a Master. True Masters are only those who have reached the Fifth Initiation of Major Mysteries. Before the Fifth Initiation nobody is a Master." - Samael Aun Weor, *The Perfect Matrimony*

Meditation: "When the esoterist submerges himself into meditation, what he seeks is information." - Samael Aun Weor

"It is urgent to know how to meditate in order to comprehend any psychic aggregate, or in other words, any psychological defect. It is indispensable to know how to work with all our heart and with all our soul, if we want the elimination to occur." - Samael Aun Weor, *The Pistis Sophia Unveiled*

"1. The Gnostic must first attain the ability to stop the course of his thoughts, the capacity to not think. Indeed, only the one who achieves that capacity will hear the Voice of the Silence.

"2. When the Gnostic disciple attains the capacity to not think, then he must learn to concentrate his thoughts on only one thing.

"3. The third step is correct meditation. This brings the first flashes of the new consciousness into the mind.

"4. The fourth step is contemplation, ecstasy or Samadhi. This is the state of Turiya (perfect clairvoyance). - Samael Aun Weor, *The Perfect Matrimony*

Monad: (Latin) From monas, "unity; a unit, monad." The Monad is the Being, the Innermost, our own inner Spirit.

"We must distinguish between Monads and Souls. A Monad, in other words, a Spirit, is; a Soul is acquired. Distinguish between the Monad of a world and the Soul of a world; between the Monad of a human and the Soul of a human; between the Monad of an ant and the Soul of an ant. The human organism, in final synthesis, is constituted by billions and trillions of infinitesimal Monads. There are several types and orders of primary elements of all existence, of every organism, in the manner of germs of all the phenomena of nature; we can call the latter Monads, employing the term of Leibnitz, in the absence of a more descriptive term to indicate the simplicity of the simplest existence. An atom, as a vehicle of action, corresponds to each of these genii or Monads. The Monads attract each other, combine, transform themselves, giving form to every organism, world, micro-organism, etc. Hierarchies exist among the Monads; the Inferior Monads must obey the Superior ones that is the Law. Inferior Monads belong to the Superior ones. All the trillions of Monads that animate the human organism have to obey the owner, the chief, the Principal Monad. The regulating Monad, the Primordial Monad permits the activity of all of its subordinates inside the human organism, until the time indicated by the Law of Karma." - Samael Aun Weor, *The Esoteric Treatise of Hermetic Astrology*

"(The number) one is the Monad, the Unity, Iod-Heve or Jehovah, the Father who is in secret. It is the Divine Triad that is not incarnated within a Master who has not killed the ego. He is Osiris, the same God, the Word." - Samael Aun Weor, *Tarot and Kabbalah*

"When spoken of, the Monad is referred to as Osiris. He is the one who has to Self-realize Himself... Our own particular Monad needs us and we need it. Once, while speaking with my Monad, my Monad told me, 'I am self-realizing Thee; what I am doing, I am doing for Thee.' Otherwise, why are we living? The Monad wants to Self-realize and that is why we are here. This is our objective." - Samael Aun Weor, *Tarot and Kabbalah*

"The Monads or Vital Genii are not exclusive to the physical organism; within the atoms of the Internal Bodies there are found imprisoned many orders and categories of living Monads. The existence of any physical or supersensible, Angelic or Diabolical, Solar or Lunar body, has billions and trillions of Monads as their foundation." - Samael Aun Weor, *The Esoteric Treatise of Hermetic Astrology*

Nirmanakaya: See: Kaya

Nirvana: (Sanskrit, "extinction"; Tibetan: nyangde, literally "the state beyond sorrow") In general use, refers to the permanent cessation of suffering and its causes, and therefore refers to a state of consciousness rather than a place. Yet, the term can also apply to heavenly realms, whose vibration is directed related to the cessation of suffering. In other words, if your mind-stream has liberated itself from the causes of suffering, it will naturally vibrate at the level of Nirvana (heaven).

"When the Soul fuses with the Inner Master, then it becomes free from Nature and enters into the supreme happiness of absolute existence. This state of happiness is called Nirvana. Nirvana can be attained through millions of births and deaths, but it can also be attained by means of a shorter path; this is the path of "initiation." The Initiate can reach Nirvana in one single life if he so wants it." - Samael Aun Weor, *The Zodiacal Course*

Objective: [See: Subjective]

Ray of Creation: The light of the Ain Soph Aur, also known as the Okidanokh, Quetzalcoatl, Kulkulcan, Krestos, and Christ. This Ray decends as a lightning bolt, creating and illuminating all the levels of existence.

"The proper arrangement of the Ray of Creation is as follows:

1. Absolute - Protocosmos
2. All the worlds from all of the clusters of Galaxies - Ayocosmos
3. A Galaxy or group of Suns - Macrocosmos
4. The Sun, Solar System - Deuterocosmos
5. The Earth, or any of the planets - Mesocosmos
6. The Philosophical Earth, Human Being - Microcosmos
7. The Abyss, Hell - Tritocosmos

"The brothers and sisters of the Gnostic Movement must deeply comprehend the esoteric knowledge which we give in this Christmas Message, in order for them to exactly know the place that they occupy in the Ray of Creation." - Samael Aun Weor, *The Elimination of Satan's Tail*

Sambogakaya: See: Kaya

Samsara: (Sanskrit; Tibetan khorwa) Cyclic, conditioned existence whose defining characteristic is suffering. It is contrasted with nirvana.

Samadhi: (Sanskrit) Literally means "union" or "combination" and its Tibetan equivilent means "adhering to that which is profound and definitive," or ting nge dzin, meaning "To hold unwaveringly, so there is no movement." Related terms include satori, ecstasy, manteia, etc. Samadhi is a state of consciousness. In the west, the term is used to describe an ecstatic state of consciousness in which the Essence escapes the painful limitations of the mind (the "I") and therefore experiences what is real: the Being, the Great Reality. There are many levels of Samadhi. In the sutras and tantras the term Samadhi has a much broader application whose precise interpretation depends upon which school and teaching is using it.

"Ecstasy is not a nebulous state, but a transcendental state of wonderment, which is associated with perfect mental clarity." - Samael Aun Weor, *The Elimination of Satan's Tail*

Self-observation: An exercise of attention, in which one learns to become an indifferent observer of one's own psychological process. True Self-observation is an active work of directed attention, without the interference of thought.

"We need attention intentionally directed towards the interior of our own selves. This is not a passive attention. Indeed, dynamic attention proceeds from the side of the observer, while thoughts and emotions belong to the side which is observed." - Samael Aun Weor, *Revolutionary Psychology*

Self-realization: The achievement of perfect knowledge. This phrase is better stated as, "The realization of the Innermost Self," or "The realization of the true nature of self." At the ultimate level, this is the experiential, conscious knowledge of the Absolute, which is synonymous with Emptiness, Shunyata, or Non-being.

Self-remembering: A state of active consciousness, controlled by will, that begins with awareness of being here and now. This state has many levels (see: Consciousness). True Self-remembering occurs without thought or mental processing: it is a state of conscious perception and includes the remembrance of the inner Being.

Solar Bodies: The physical, vital, astral, mental, and casual bodies that are created through the beginning stages of Alchemy/Tantra and that provide a basis for existence in their corresponding levels of nature, just as the physical body does in the physical world. These bodies or vehicles are superior due to being created out of Solar (Christic) Energy, as opposed to the inferior, lunar bodies we receive from nature. Also known as the Wedding Garment (Christianity), the Merkabah (Kabbalah), To Soma Heliakon (Greek), and Sahu (Egyptian).

"All the Masters of the White Lodge, the Angels, Archangels, Thrones, Seraphim, Virtues, etc., etc., etc. are garbed with the Solar Bodies. Only those who have Solar Bodies have the Being incarnated. Only someone who possesses the Being is an authentic Human Being." - Samael Aun Weor, *The Esoteric Treatise of Hermetic Astrology*

Subjective: "What do modern psychologists understand as 'objective?' They understand it to be that which is external to the mind: the physical, the tangible, the material.

"Yet, they are totally mistaken, because when analysing the term "subjective," we see that it signifies "sub, under," that which is below the range

of our perceptions. What is below our perceptions? Is it not perhaps the
Infernal Worlds? Is it not perhaps subjective that which is in the physical
or beneath the physical? So, what is truly subjective is what is below the
limits of our perceptions.

"Psychologists do not know how to use the former terms correctly.

"Objective: the light, the resplendence; it is that which contains the
Truth, clarity, lucidity.

"Subjective: the darkness, the tenebrous. The subjective elements of
perception are the outcome of seeing, hearing, touching, smelling and
tasting. All of these are perceptions of what we see in the third dimension. For example, in one cube we see only length, width and height. We
do not see the fourth dimension because we are bottled up within the
ego. The subjective elements of perception are constituted by the ego
with all of its "I's." - Samael Aun Weor, *The Initiatic Path in the Arcana of
Tarot and Kabbalah*

Yoga: (Sanskrit) "union." Similar to the Latin "religare," the root of the
word "religion." In Tibetan, it is "rnal-'byor" which means "union with
the fundamental nature of reality."

"The word YOGA comes from the root Yuj which means to join, and in
its spiritual sense, it is that process by which the human spirit is brought
into near and conscious communion with, or is merged in, the Divine
Spirit, according as the nature of the human spirit is held to be separate
from (Dvaita, Visishtadvaita) or one with (Advaita) the Divine Spirit." -
Swami Sivananda, *Kundalini Yoga*

"Patanjali defines Yoga as the suspension of all the functions of the mind.
As such, any book on Yoga, which does not deal with these three aspects
of the subject, viz., mind, its functions and the method of suspending
them, can he safely laid aside as unreliable and incomplete." - Swami
Sivananda, *Practical Lessons In Yoga*

"The word yoga means in general to join one's mind with an actual fact..."
- The 14th Dalai Lama

"The soul aspires for the union with his Innermost, and the Innermost
aspires for the union with his Glorian." - Samael Aun Weor, *The Revolution of Beelzebub*

"All of the seven schools of Yoga are within Gnosis, yet they are in a synthesized and absolutely practical way. There is Tantric Hatha Yoga in the
practices of the Maithuna (Sexual Magic). There is practical Raja Yoga in
the work with the chakras. There is Gnana Yoga in our practices and mental disciplines which we have cultivated in secrecy for millions of years.
We have Bhakti Yoga in our prayers and Rituals. We have Laya Yoga in
our meditation and respiratory exercises. Samadhi exists in our practices
with the Maithuna and during our deep meditations. We live the path
of Karma Yoga in our upright actions, in our upright thoughts, in our
upright feelings, etc." - Samael Aun Weor, *The Revolution of Beelzebub*

"The Yoga that we require today is actually ancient Gnostic Christian Yoga, which absolutely rejects the idea of Hatha Yoga. We do not recommend Hatha Yoga simply because, spiritually speaking, the acrobatics of this discipline are fruitless; they should be left to the acrobats of the circus." - Samael Aun Weor, *The Yellow Book*

"Yoga has been taught very badly in the Western World. Multitudes of pseudo-sapient Yogis have spread the false belief that the true Yogi must be an infrasexual (an enemy of sex). Some of these false yogis have never even visited India; they are infrasexual pseudo-yogis. These ignoramuses believe that they are going to achieve in-depth realization only with the yogic exercises, such as asanas, pranayamas, etc. Not only do they have such false beliefs, but what is worse is that they propagate them; thus, they misguide many people away from the difficult, straight, and narrow door that leads unto the light. No authentically Initiated Yogi from India would ever think that he could achieve his inner self-realization with pranayamas or asanas, etc. Any legitimate Yogi from India knows very well that such yogic exercises are only co-assistants that are very useful for their health and for the development of their powers, etc. Only the Westerners and pseudo-yogis have within their minds the belief that they can achieve Self-realization with such exercises.Sexual Magic is practiced very secretly within the Ashrams of India. Any True Yogi Initiate from India works with the Arcanum A.Z.F. This is taught by the Great Yogis from India that have visited the Western world, and if it has not been taught by these great, Initiated Hindustani Yogis, if it has not been published in their books of Yoga, it was in order to avoid scandals. You can be absolutely sure that the Yogis who do not practice Sexual Magic will never achieve birth in the Superior Worlds. Thus, whosoever affirms the contrary is a liar, an impostor." - Samael Aun Weor, *The Estoeric Course of Kabbalah*

Yogi: (Sanskrit) male yoga practitioner.

Yogini: (Sanskrit) female yoga practitioner.

Index

Pines, 57
Plane, 92, 111-112
Planes, 91, 126, 132, 135
Planet, 4, 15, 18, 57-58, 89, 121, 144, 156
Planetary, 91-92
Planets, 57, 92
Plant, 14-16, 121, 129, 148
Plants, 4, 14, 16, 44, 57, 66, 148
Plato, 130
Pleasure, 17, 30, 34-36, 47, 55, 59, 79, 90, 170
Plexus, 63
Pluralized, 115, 131-132, 151
Pluto, 147
Police, 35, 40-41
Policeman, 123
Politicians, 61
Position, 134
Positive, 141, 168
Positivist, 121
Power, 36, 44, 69, 72, 75, 79, 105-107, 109, 117, 123-124, 134, 153-154
Powers, 71, 79, 97, 105-106, 109, 117, 154
Practical, 48, 71, 73, 90, 123, 135, 153
Practical Magic, 71, 73, 90
Practice, 61, 70, 99, 167
Practices, 57, 98
Pray, 11, 40-41, 43, 52, 55, 65, 80, 110-111
Prayers, 5, 51, 54, 61
Pre-columbian, 62
Predestination, 14
Pregnancy, 78
Presidents, 92
Pride, 93, 140, 151
Priest, 61, 84, 123, 142
Priests, 44, 53, 161
Prince Siddhartha, 155
Princes, 144
Princes of Fire, 144
Princess, 78, 84, 86
Principal, 135, 151
Principalities, 144

Principle, 7, 115, 159
Principles, 147, 158
Prisoner, 97
Prisoners, 61, 66
Problem, 33, 36, 48, 67, 89, 152, 163, 166
Problems, 26, 48, 68-69, 78, 157
Project, 45, 47, 50, 133
Projected, 43, 45, 47, 49, 57
Projection, 39, 41, 45, 47, 49-50, 52, 57
Projects, 50, 133
Prophecy, 36
Prophesied, 111
Prophesy, 111
Prophet, 109, 111
Prostate, 107
Protestant, 78
Protons, 139
Protoplasm, 28
Pseudo-esoteric, 70
Pseudo-occultist, 70
Psyche, 41, 149, 152-154, 157
Psychiatrists, 36
Psychic, 7, 30, 59, 76, 129, 155
Psychological, 9, 143, 153, 155-156
Psychology, 144-145, 150, 153
Pulmonary, 115
Punishment, 13, 24-25, 67-68, 76, 129, 144-146
Pure, 14, 23, 53, 80-81, 103, 132, 169
Purest, 131, 158
Purgatory, 19
Purification, 19, 73, 82, 103, 145-146
Purity, 17
Pygmies, 58-59
Pyramids, 60-61, 160, 168
Pythagoras, 159
Pythoness, 69
Quarks, 139
Queen, 147
Races, 58
Radiate, 156
Radiates, 139
Radioactive, 131
RAOM GAOM, 98
Raphael, 72, 75

White Brotherhood, 72
White Lodge, 124, 133
Whore, 9
Wife, 9, 23-25, 39, 48, 58, 78, 97
Wine, 83
Winter, 21
Wireless, 63
Wisdom, 49, 53, 83, 93, 122, 159,
   168
Wise, 19, 24, 71, 77, 105-106, 109,
   111
Witchcraft, 24, 67-68, 77
Wizards, 69
Wolf, 101
Woman, 27, 29-30, 35-36, 48, 67-68,
   105, 115, 166
Womanizer, 9
Womb, 4-5, 13, 91, 97, 105-106, 130,
   143, 166
Wombs, 165-167
Women, 9, 15, 29, 68, 105, 166
Word, 4, 14, 20-21, 34, 51, 66, 82-83,
   141, 145, 147, 156
Words, 20, 28, 35, 43, 52, 54, 58,
   80-82, 98, 109, 143, 159, 164,
   169-170
Worship, 141, 156
Worshipped, 156
Worshipping, 141
Yellow, 52, 54
Yod-HaVah, 72
Yoga, 130, 135
Yogi, 106, 168
Yogic, 53
Young, 11, 27, 30, 34-36, 45, 47, 50,
   76-78, 85, 164
Youth, 58, 119
Zachariel, 72
Zarahiel, 72
Zodiacal, 91
Zodiacal Course, 91
Zoosperm, 122, 130
Zoroaster, 91, 132

Glorian Publishing is a non-profit publisher dedicated to spreading the sacred universal doctrine to suffering humanity. All of our works are made possible by the kindness and generosity of sponsors. If you would like to make a tax-deductible donation, you may send it to the address below, or visit our website for other alternatives. If you would like to sponsor the publication of a book, please contact us at 877-726-2359 or help@gnosticteachings.org.

Glorian Publishing
PO Box 110225
Brooklyn, NY 11211 US
Phone: 877-726-2359

VISIT US ONLINE AT:

glorian.info
gnosticbooks.org
gnosticteachings.org
gnosticradio.org
gnosticstore.org